SPANISH
AND MEXICAN
COOKING

Marshall Cavendish London & New York

Picture Credits:
Colorific/M. Desjardins 2/3;
Alan Duns 10, 16, 17, 30, 57;
Paul Kemp 52, 56;
Don Last 39;
John Lees 63;
David Meldrum 33;
Toby Molenaar 1;
Stanli Opperman 51;
Roger Phillips 6/7, 8, 13, 15, 18, 19, 20, 22/3, 25, 26, 34, 40,
41, 43, 44, 47, 48, 50, 59, 61, 62;
Iain Reid 5, 29, 36, 55, 58, 60.

Cover: Roger Phillips

Written and edited by Isabel Moore

Published by
Marshall Cavendish Books Limited
58 Old Compton Street
London W1V 5PA

© Marshall Cavendish Limited 1973, 1974, 1975, 1977

Parts of this material first published by Marshall
Cavendish Limited in the partwork *Supercook*

This volume first published 1977

Printed in Great Britain by Redwood Burn Limited
Trowbridge & Esher

ISBN 0 85685 255 4

Contents

Introduction

Spain and Mexico are literally oceans apart. But the Spanish conquest of Mexico over 300 years ago has assured some similarities—the language and religion are the same, and they share an enthusiasm for bull-fighting, guitars and long, lazy siestas. And *machismo*, it is worth noting, is also a Spanish word, applicable equally to the old country and the new. There is also a common interest in food: before the conquest, the Mexicans boiled everything, existing on a diet which consisted mainly of corn, potatoes, tomatoes and chocolate, all liberally laced with highly potent chillis; now they fry most things and live on a diet of corn, potatoes, tomatoes and chocolate, all liberally laced with highly potent chillis. Spain did, however, contribute lard to make the frying easier.

Spanish cuisine is sadly under-rated. Those who dismiss it as 'greasy, oily muck' are probably those who have suffered from package holiday hotel food, a situation almost guaranteed to produce gastronomical disasters in most countries. The true cuisine owes much to Spain's geographical position as co-inhabitor of the land mass in south-western Europe known as the Iberian Peninsula. Bordered as it is on three sides by the ocean, fish forms an important part of the diet, and the cuisine in general is plain and uncluttered, relying on good-quality fresh products for its excellence. Olive oil is used almost exclusively as a cooking agent—rather understandably since Spain is the largest producer of that commodity in the world.

The foundations of modern Spanish cuisine were laid down by the Romans, who conquered Spain and brought with them olive trees and garlic. Of the later conquerors, the most important were the Moors, a mixtures of tribes from northern Africa, who dominated southern Spain for over seven hundred years and who left behind them not only cities of unsurpassed beauty but a national taste for saffron, citrus fruit and nuts, especially pine nuts.

For most of its history, Spain has been a conglomeration of rival kingdoms, roughly corresponding to the present-day regions,

The general store plus client of a small, rural town in Mexico. It will often be the only shop for miles around and stock everything from safety pins to broom sticks.

so that cultural and gastronomic development have taken place separately rather than together. As a result, there is no acknowledged 'national' cuisine, although the better-known dishes from one region have, of course, travelled to and been incorporated into the eating habits of many others.

The northeastern borders with France house two of the most important of these regional cuisines, the Basque and the Catalan. In both areas live people who have their own language, customs and habits which seem unrelated to those of the rest of Spain, and in both there is a distinct cultivation of this 'separate' identity. The coastline of the Basque provinces yields an abundance of fish and it is therefore in the cooking of this food that the reputation of the excellence of Basque cooking is based. But cooking in general is an occupation which is treated with great seriousness (and because of this has traditionally been dominated by men in Basque society); all of the leading cities of the province boast all-male gastronomic societies, where the traditions of excellence are fiercely upheld—as is the unisexual nature of the institutions. In Catalonia, the tradition is also strong and the cuisine is somewhat similar to that of France, with an emphasis on sauces and herbs.

To the south of Catalonia and the Basque provinces are Castile and Aragon, famous in history as the dual kingdom ruled over by Ferdinand and Isabella. In Castile, there is the Rioja, the main wine-producing area of Spain, and certainly the best. The full-bodied red wines of the region, particularly, age beautifully, travel well and are among the relatively few Spanish wines not dismissed by the experts as *vin très ordinaire*. In Castile too, there is the region called La Mancha, the setting of Cervantes' novel *Don Quixote*. In the novel, mention is made of a medieval stew/soup called Olla Podrida (page 28), which survives today although it is now sometimes known as Cocido Madrileño. Aragon is the home of another of those famous Spanish stew/soups—this one called Fabada (page 27).

Galicia and Asturias are the other northern provinces, over on the western side just above Portugal. Galicia is bordered on two sides by the ocean and because of this, fish features prominently in the cuisine. The food tends to the hearty and uncomplicated and there are many robust and filling soups. Galicia is also the home of the Spanish Empanada (page 32)—not to be confused

with the smaller, spicier Mexican version—which is a filling double-crust pie filled with practically anything that takes your fancy.

Andalusia in the south is the tourist 'dream' of Spain, all dusty, forgotten Moorish castles, melancholy guitar music and the lost, haunted sound and rhythm of the flamenco. It was here that the Moorish influence was strongest, and can still be seen. It lingers in the construction of some of the older cities, and in the cultivation of oranges, a fruit introduced by the Moors and which is now one of the main crops of the region. Andalusia is also the home of the Paella, although that dish is probably the nearest the Spaniards have to a national dish and versions of it are found in many other provinces, and of sherry, a fortified wine which owes its name to foreign inability to pronounce the name of the city from which it comes, Jerez.

Although its origins are as ancient as those of Spain, Mexico is part of the New World. It occupies a prominent position on the Central American Peninsula, north of Guatemala and Honduras, south of the

southwestern states of the United States. It is a country created by a series of highly advanced Indian civilizations, which until the early sixteenth century had never seen a white man.

In 1519 all that was changed when Hernando Cortès, a native of Extremadura in western Spain, marched into Tenochtitlan (modern-day Mexico City), then the largest city in the world and the capital of the Aztec empire. The Aztec leader, called Montezuma, in his innocence thought of the Spaniards as special pale gods. The Spaniards in their wisdom thought Mexico an uncivilized land inhabited by primitive pagans and ripe only for plunder. But while their main concern was for gold and other precious metals, some of that plunder did take rather an unusual form: chocolate, tomatoes, corn and capsicums were all native to Mexico and all were unknown in Europe until taken back by the *conquistadors*.

The basis of Mexican cuisine, both before and after the Spanish conquest, was corn, a plant sacred to the Aztecs and possibly to the Mayas before them. It was used in many ways but most importantly to make the flat unleavened bread called tortilla, which is still widely used in Mexico today both as a bread and as the basis for many savoury snack dishes. Originally cooked on a sort of flat griddle called a *comal*, now—the price of progress—it is more usually manufactured on special tortilla-making machines. No part of the ear of corn was wasted; even the outer husks were used (and still are) in making *tamales*, little parcels of corn dough stuffed with mixtures such as Picadillo (page 17) or Frijoles Refritos (page 51) and then tucked into the husks. In earliest times, the husks were usually cooked over an open fire; nowadays they are more likely to be thrust into a colander and steamed in a pan of boiling water.

Chillis were used by all of the Indian civilizations of Central and South America but nowhere did they become as popular as in Mexico. Over thirty varieties are used there, ranging from mild to pretty lethal. Some are merely local varieties, unobtainable outside their narrow region, others are available and used widely throughout the world. Most Mexican food is very hot, so the recipes in this book, while every endeavour has been made to assure their authenticity, have been scaled down in 'heat' slightly as an act of kindness to protect the non-Mexican palate!

Mexican food, like Spanish, does vary quite widely from region to region, although there are some standard dishes that are found throughout the country. Where the regional differences occur, they are often due to geographical conditions: in Yucatan, for instance, much of the province is bound by the sea and fish therefore figures largely in the local diet. In the states which border on the United States, with access to the cattle country there and with a similar geography, meat, particularly beef, is favoured and many of the dishes owe much to Texas and the outdoor way of life. In Jalisco province, the plant called *aguey* is grown which, when refined and fermented, becomes the great white spirit of Mexico, *tequila*. Although it has the reputation of having a powerful 'kick' to it, commercial varieties are in fact usually no stronger than whisky.

Both cuisines offer enormous range and variety of eating pleasure and both particularly suit the modern way of life in that complicated dishes requiring much preparation and careful cooking are on the whole avoided.

Soups and Dips

SOPA DE ALBONDIGAS
(Meatball Soup)

This spicy Mexican soup is traditionally served with hot tortillas. A clear consommé base may be substituted for the tomato one used here and ½ teaspoon of hot chilli powder may be substituted for the chilli pepper.

	Metric/U.K.	U.S.
Butter	25g/1oz	2 Tbs
Onion, chopped	1	1
Small dried hot red chillis, crumbled	2	2
Dried oregano	½ tsp	½ tsp
Tomatoes, blanched, peeled and puréed	1kg/2lb	2lb
Water	1¼l/2pints	5 cups
Salt	1½ tsp	1½ tsp
MEATBALLS		
Minced (ground) beef	350g/12oz	12oz
Cooked rice	4 Tbs	4 Tbs
Small onion, grated	1	1
Small egg	1	1
Ground cumin	¼ tsp	¼ tsp
Finely chopped coriander leaves	1 tsp	1 tsp
Salt and pepper to taste		

Melt the butter in a large saucepan. Add the onion and fry until it is soft. Stir in the chillis and oregano and cook for 30 seconds. Stir in the tomatoes and water and add the salt. Bring to the boil and cook, uncovered, for 1 hour, or until the liquid has reduced by about half.

Meanwhile, combine all the meatball ingredients in a large bowl. Using your hands, roll the mixture into small, walnut-sized balls. Add the balls to the soup. Reduce the heat to low, cover and simmer the soup for 40 minutes, or until the meatballs are cooked through.

Transfer the mixture to a warmed tureen and serve at once.

6 Servings

CALDO DE CONGRIO
(Conger Eel Soup)

Spain has an abundance of seafood and many interesting dishes with a fish base. This particular soup is rich and filling and almost makes a meal in itself. Any firm, white-fleshed fish may be substituted for the eel, although the latter is the traditional main ingredient.

	Metric/U.K.	U.S.
Olive oil	1½ Tbs	1½ Tbs
Medium onions, sliced	3	3
Garlic clove, crushed	1	1
Tomatoes, blanched, peeled, seeded and chopped	700g/1½lb	1½lb
Tomato purée (paste)	1 Tbs	1 Tbs
Dried oregano	½ tsp	½ tsp
Bay leaf	1	1
Salt and pepper to taste		
Potatoes, cut into 1cm/½ in wide strips	½kg/1lb	1lb
Fish stock	900ml/1½ pints	3¾ cups
Conger eel, cleaned and cut into 5cm/2in steaks	1 × 3kg/6lb	1 × 6lb
Ground coriander	1 tsp	1 tsp
Finely chopped parsley	2 Tbs	2 Tbs

Heat the oil in a large saucepan. Add the onions and garlic and fry until they are soft. Add the tomatoes, tomato purée (paste), oregano, bay leaf and seasoning and cook for 5 minutes, stirring constantly. Add the potatoes and fish stock and bring to the boil. Reduce the heat to low, cover and simmer the soup for 20 minutes.

Stir in the eel steaks and coriander. Re-cover and simmer for a further 12 minutes, or until the eel flesh flakes easily, and the potatoes are cooked and tender. Remove and discard the bay leaf.

Transfer the soup to a warmed tureen, sprinkle over the parsley and serve at once.

8 Servings

ESCUDELLA A LA CATALANA
(Catalan Sausage and Vegetable Soup)

This sturdy soup is from Catalonia and can be served as a meal in itself, with lots of crusty bread.

	Metric/U.K.	U.S.
Beef stock	1¾l/3 pints	7½ cups
Large potatoes, diced	2	2
Carrots, diced	3	3
Turnip, diced	1	1
Onion, chopped	1	1
Garlic cloves, crushed	2	2
Celery stalks, chopped	2	2
Salt and pepper to taste		
Bay leaf	1	1
Long-grain rice, soaked in cold water for 30 minutes and drained	2 Tbs	2 Tbs
Ground saffron	¼ tsp	¼ tsp
Chorizo sausage, thinly sliced	175g/6oz	6oz

Pour the stock into a large saucepan and bring to the boil. Add the vegetables, seasoning and bay leaf and bring to the boil again. Reduce the heat to low, cover the pan and simmer for 30 minutes.

Add the rice, saffron and sausage and simmer for a further 15 to 20 minutes, or until the rice is cooked. Remove from the heat and remove and discard the bay leaf.

Transfer to a warmed tureen and serve at once.

6 Servings

Spain is noted for her filling, delicious soups and Escudella a la Catalana, a mixture of vegetables and sausage, is one of the best.

CALDO HABA
(Broad [Fava or Lima] Bean Soup)

This hearty, filling soup contains the popular Spanish ingredients of broad (fava or lima) beans, Serrano ham and chorizo sausage. If you cannot obtain Serrano, any other type of ham may be substituted.

	Metric/U.K.	U.S.
Water	2½l/4 pints	5 pints
Broad beans (fava or lima beans), soaked in cold water overnight and drained	225g/8oz	1⅓ cups
Serrano ham	225g/8oz	8oz
Medium onion, chopped	1	1
Salt and pepper to taste		
Chorizo sausage	175g/6oz	6oz
Small turnip, chopped	1	1
Potatoes, chopped	2	2

Pour the water into a large saucepan and add the beans. Bring to the boil and boil for 2 minutes, skimming any scum from the surface of the soup. Cover the pan, remove from the heat and set aside for 1½ hours.

Return the pan to the heat and add the ham, onion and seasoning. Bring to the boil, skimming off any scum which rises to the surface. Reduce the heat to low, half-cover the pan and simmer for 1½ hours.

Prick the chorizo in one or two places with a fork and add to the soup with the remaining ingredients. Simmer for a further 30 minutes or until the potatoes are cooked and tender.

Using a slotted spoon, transfer the ham and chorizo to a chopping board and, when they are cool enough to handle, cut them into bite-sized pieces. Return them to the soup and simmer gently until they are heated through.

Transfer to a warmed tureen and serve at once.

6 Servings

CALDO TLALPENO
(Chicken and Bean Soup)

This Mexican soup contains an unusual mixture of ingredients, including avocado and cheese.

Any firm white cheese will do, such as Cheddar or California jack. Serve with hot tortillas for an authentic touch.

	Metric/U.K.	U.S.
Boiling chicken	1 × 2½kg/5lb	1 × 5lb
Medium onion, quartered	1	1
Carrot, sliced	1	1
Salt	2 tsp	2 tsp
Peppercorns	4	4
Bouquet garni	1	1
Water	3l/5 pints	6 pints

Green peppers, pith and seeds removed and sliced	2	2
Large onion, thinly sliced into rings	1	1
Canned chick-peas, drained	425g/14oz	14oz
Black pepper	$\frac{1}{4}$ tsp	$\frac{1}{4}$ tsp
Firm white cheese, cubed	225g/8oz	8oz
Avocado, peeled, stoned, sliced and sprinkled with lemon juice	1	1

Put the chicken into a large saucepan and add the quartered onion, carrot, 1 teaspoon of salt, the peppercorns and bouquet garni. Pour over the water, adding more if necessary to cover the chicken completely. Bring to the boil, then reduce the heat to moderately low and simmer the chicken for 2 hours, or until it is cooked through and tender. Remove the chicken from the pan and transfer to a chopping board. Cover with foil to keep hot.

Increase the heat to moderately high and bring the pan liquid to the boil. Boil for 15 minutes, or until it has reduced slightly. Strain, discarding the contents of the strainer. Rinse out the saucepan and return the strained liquid to it. Return to the boil, skimming off

Caldo Tlalpeno is a traditional Mexican soup whose basic ingredients are chicken, beans and avocado.

One of the most famous of Spanish classics, Gazpacho — a delicious soup served cold with a variety of garnishes.

any scum which rises to the surface. Add the sliced peppers and onion rings, reduce the heat to moderately low and simmer for 10 minutes. Stir in the chick-peas and simmer for a further 5 minutes.

Meanwhile, cut the chicken into serving pieces and return to the saucepan. Add the remaining salt and the pepper and simmer for a further 5 minutes, or until the chicken pieces are heated through. Stir in the cheese cubes.

As soon as the cheese melts, transfer the soup to a warmed tureen and add the avocado slices. Serve at once.

6–8 Servings

SOPA DE AJO CON HUEVOS
(Garlic Soup with Eggs)

This is a Spanish classic, found throughout the

country and with almost as many versions as there are regions. At its simplest, it is bread and garlic fried in oil with water added. This version adds tomatoes and beaten eggs, and is one of the most popular variations on the theme.

	Metric/U.K.	U.S.
Olive oil	50ml/2floz	¼ cup
Garlic cloves, chopped	4	4
French or Italian bread, crusts removed and cubed or chopped	4 slices	4 slices
Paprika	1 tsp	1 tsp
Salt and pepper to taste		
Water	1¼l/2 pints	5 cups
Tomatoes, blanched, peeled and chopped	3	3
Eggs, lightly beaten	2	2

Heat the oil in a large saucepan. Add the

garlic and fry for 2 minutes, stirring constantly. Add the bread pieces and fry until they are lightly and evenly browned. Stir in the paprika and seasoning, then pour over the water and tomatoes. Bring to the boil, reduce the heat to low and cover the pan. Simmer for 15 to 20 minutes, or until the bread is very soft, and beginning to break up.

Carefully pour in the beaten eggs, in a steady stream, and simmer gently for about 1 minute, taking care not to let the soup come to the boil or the eggs will curdle. Serve at once.

4–6 Servings

SOPA AL CUARTO DE HORA
(Quarter-of-an-Hour Soup)

This quaintly named Spanish soup is a filling mixture of seafood, ham and vegetables. It is so named because the main stage of cooking takes quarter of an hour.

	Metric/U.K.	U.S.
Water	900ml/1½ pints	3¾ cups
Small clams, scrubbed	6	6
Olive oil	2 Tbs	2 Tbs
Medium onion, chopped	1	1
Garlic clove, crushed	1	1
Tomatoes, blanched, peeled and chopped	2	2
Long-grain rice, soaked in cold water for 30 minutes and drained	25g/1oz	⅙ cup
Lemon juice	1 Tbs	1 Tbs
Shelled shrimps	225g/8oz	8oz
Serrano or other ham, chopped	50g/2oz	2oz
Hard-boiled egg, finely chopped	1	1

Pour the water into a large saucepan and bring to the boil. Add the clams, cover and cook for 6 to 8 minutes, or until the shells open (discard any clams that do not open). Using a slotted spoon, transfer the clams to a serving plate and keep hot. Either remove one or both shells, according to taste. Reserve the clam cooking liquid.

Heat the oil in a small saucepan. Add the onion and garlic and fry until they are soft. Stir in the tomatoes and fry gently until the mixture is thick and pulpy. Remove from the heat.

Strain the clam liquid into a fresh saucepan, and bring to the boil. Stir in the tomato mixture, rice and lemon juice, and bring to the boil again. Reduce the heat to low and simmer the soup for 15 minutes.

Stir in the remaining ingredients, including the reserved clams, and simmer for a further 2 to 3 minutes, or until the shrimps and clams are heated through.

Transfer the soup to a warmed tureen and serve at once.

6 Servings

GAZPACHO
(Chilled Tomato Soup)

There are many versions of what is perhaps one of the two or three Spanish 'classic' dishes. This is a simple, basic version. It is traditionally served with a variety of accompaniments, such as croûtons, chopped olives, cucumbers, hardboiled eggs and onions. Each diner sprinkles a little of the accompaniments over his Gazpacho before eating.

	Metric/U.K.	U.S.
Brown bread, cut into cubes	3 slices	3 slices
Canned tomato juice	300ml/10floz	1¼ cups
Garlic cloves, crushed	2	2
Cucumber, peeled and finely chopped	½	½
Green pepper, pith and seeds removed and chopped	1	1
Red pepper, pith and seeds removed and chopped	1	1
Large onion, chopped	1	1
Tomatoes, blanched, peeled and chopped	700g/1½lb	1½lb
Olive oil	75ml/3floz	⅜ cup
Red wine vinegar	2 Tbs	2 Tbs
Salt and pepper to taste		
Dried marjoram	¼ tsp	¼ tsp
Dried basil	¼ tsp	¼ tsp

	Metric/U.K.	U.S.
Ice cubes (optional)	4	4

Put the bread cubes in a bowl and pour over the tomato juice. Leave to soak for 5 minutes, then squeeze to extract the excess juice. Transfer to a large bowl and reserve the juice.

Add the garlic, cucumber, peppers, onion and tomatoes to the soaked bread and stir to mix. Put the mixture into a blender and blend to a smooth paste, or push through a food mill until the mixture is smooth. Stir in the reserved tomato juice.

Add all the remaining ingredients, except the ice cubes, to the mixture and stir well. The soup should be the consistency of single (light) cream so add more tomato juice if necessary.

Transfer the soup to a deep serving bowl and chill in the refrigerator for 1 hour. Just before serving, stir well and float in the ice cubes, if you are using them.

Guacamole is a traditional Mexican dip based on avocado.

4–6 Servings

GUACAMOLE
(Avocado Dip)

This is one of the most popular of Mexican dishes and is almost as well-known outside the country as inside. It is much easier and quicker to make if you have a blender, but the traditional method of putting it together is given below. Serve with a variety of raw vegetables.

	Metric/U.K.	U.S.
Medium ripe avocados	3	3
Lemon juice	1 Tbs	1 Tbs
Olive oil	2 tsp	2 tsp
Salt and pepper to taste		
Ground coriander	½ tsp	½ tsp
Hard-boiled egg, chopped	1	1
Small green pepper, pith and seeds removed and chopped	½	½

Small dried hot red chillis, crumbled	1½	1½
Spring onions (scallions), chopped	2	2
Tomato, blanched, peeled, seeded and chopped	1	1

Halve the avocados and remove the stones. Peel and transfer the flesh to a large bowl. Mash with a fork until it is smooth, then gradually beat in the lemon juice, olive oil, seasoning and coriander. Beat in all the remaining ingredients. Chill in the refrigerator for 1 hour.

Transfer the mixture to a serving bowl and serve at once if possible.

4–6 Servings

SALSA DE CHILE ROJO
(Red Chilli Sauce)

There are several distinctive types of chilli used in Mexican cooking, ranging from mild to fiery hot. The types most usually used in this classic sauce are ancho, *a mild but pungent chilli or* péquin *a small, much hotter variety. Péquin or other small dried red chilli has been suggested for the recipe given below, but if you prefer to substitute* ancho *chillis, double the quantity and soak them in boiling water for 30 minutes before draining and using. This sauce is used in many ways—as an accompaniment to tortillas, tacos, or enchiladas, or either served with meat and poultry or cooked with them.*

	Metric/U.K.	U.S.
Small dried red *péquin* or other similar chillis, crumbled	5	5
Boiling water	3 Tbs	3 Tbs
Canned peeled tomatoes, chopped and drained but with the juice reserved	425g/14oz	14oz
Vegetable oil	50ml/2floz	¼ cup
Onion, chopped	1	1
Garlic cloves, crushed	2	2
Tomato purée (paste)	2 Tbs	2 Tbs
Ground cumin	1 tsp	1 tsp
Wine vinegar	1½ Tbs	1½ Tbs
Sugar	½ tsp	½ tsp

Put the chillis, water and chopped tomatoes into a blender and blend to a smooth purée. Pour into a jug and set aside.

Heat the oil in a saucepan. Add the onion and garlic and fry until they are soft. Stir in the tomato mixture, the reserved tomato can juice and the remaining ingredients, and bring to the boil. Reduce the heat to low, cover and simmer the sauce for 10 minutes.

The sauce is now ready to be added to other ingredients, or to be served.

About 600ml/1 pint (2½ cups)

SALSA DE TOMATILLO VERDE
(Green Tomato Sauce)

This unusual sauce is a popular accompaniment to tortilla dishes in Mexico, particularly tacos and enchiladas, but it could also be used as an accompaniment to roast or grilled (broiled) meat, particularly lamb. Canned green tomatoes are available from Mexican provision stores.

	Metric/U.K.	U.S.
Vegetable oil	2 Tbs	2 Tbs
Large onion, chopped	1	1
Canned Mexican green tomatoes	450g/1lb	1lb
Canned green chillis, drained and chopped	2	2
Finely chopped coriander leaves	1 Tbs	1 Tbs
Chicken stock	250ml/8floz	1 cup

Heat the oil in a small frying-pan. Add the onion and fry until it is soft. Remove from the heat.

Put the onion, tomatoes and can juice, chillis and coriander leaves into a blender and blend to a smooth purée. Pour into a saucepan and set over low heat. Gradually add the chicken stock, stirring constantly. Cook until the sauce comes to the boil. Reduce the heat to low and simmer the sauce for 5 minutes.

The sauce is now ready to be added to other ingredients, or to be served.

About 725ml/25floz (3 cups)

Tortillas

Tacos filled with chilli sauce and meat is one fabulous way to make a meal of tortillas. You can either buy the tacos ready-made, or fry canned tortillas — or even make your own.

TORTILLAS
(Flat Corn Bread)

Tortillas were popular in Mexico long before the Spaniards arrived, and they have remained one of the staple foods ever since. They are traditionally made on a clay griddle called a comal, although below a frying-pan is recommended for obvious reasons. The masa harina suggested below is the type of corn meal flour usually used for making tortillas and can be obtained from Mexican and some Spanish provision stores.

	Metric/U.K.	U.S.
Masa harina (corn-meal flour)	225g/8oz	2 cups
Lukewarm water	300ml/10floz	1¼ cups

Put the masa harina into a bowl and gradually beat in the water until the mixture is well blended. Using your hands, knead the dough until it is smooth and elastic. Divide the dough into 12 equal pieces.

Put each piece between two large pieces of greaseproof or waxed paper and lay on a flat surface. Using a rolling pin, carefully roll out the dough until it is about $\frac{1}{8}$cm/$\frac{1}{16}$in thick and about 15cm/6in in diameter. Trim the dough into shape if necessary. As each piece is rolled out put to one side, still between the paper.

To cook the tortillas, heat an ungreased heavy-based frying-pan over moderate heat. Peel off the greaseproof or waxed paper from one side of one tortilla and put it, paper side up, into the pan. Cook for about 1½ minutes or until it becomes lightly speckled. Peel off the remaining paper, turn over the tortilla and cook on the second side for 1½ minutes, or until the underside is lightly browned. Wrap in a hot towel or foil and keep hot while you cook the remaining tortillas in the same way. Serve hot. (The tortillas may be cooked ahead of time, especially if they are to be served with fillings such as tacos or enchiladas; in this case, when you wish to reheat the tortillas just follow the instructions in the respective recipes.)

12 Tortillas

HUEVOS RANCHEROS
(Ranch-Style Eggs)

This classic Mexican dish is often served with Frijoles Refritos (page 51) for a filling meal.

	Metric/U.K.	U.S.
Vegetable oil	1 Tbs	1 Tbs
Tortillas	6	6
Salsa de Chile Rojo (red chilli sauce) (page 11)	450ml/15floz	2 cups
Fried eggs, kept hot	6	6
Avocado, peeled, stoned and thinly sliced	1	1

Brush a large frying-pan with some of the oil and heat over moderate heat. Holding a tortilla between your finger and thumb, dip it into the chilli sauce, shaking off any excess. Carefully arrange the tortilla in the hot frying-pan and fry for 1 to 2 minutes on each side or until it is golden brown. Using a spatula or tongs, transfer the tortilla to a large serving platter or individual serving plate and keep hot while you cook the remaining tortillas in the same way.

Pour a little of the remaining sauce over the tortillas and top each one with a fried egg. Garnish with the avocado slices. Pour the remaining sauce into a warmed sauceboat and serve at once, with the tortillas and eggs.

6 Servings

TACOS WITH CHILLI SAUCE AND MEAT FILLING

Tacos are just shaped, filled tortillas and although the most popular type is the U or half-moon shaped taco, you can, if you prefer, roll or fold the tortillas around the filling. Garnishes are also traditional and many can be used in addition to those suggested below—sliced avocado or grated cheese, for instance. Although we have suggested frying tortillas into taco shapes below, you can buy prepared tacos which have already been fried and shaped.

	Metric/U.K.	U.S.
Sufficient oil for shallow-frying		
Tortillas	12	12

SAUCE FILLING		
Vegetable oil	50ml/2floz	¼ cup
Small onion, chopped	1	1
Minced (ground) beef	½kg/1lb	1lb
Salsa de Chile Rojo (red chilli sauce) (page 11)	450ml/15floz	2 cups
GARNISHES		
Tomatoes, finely chopped	4	4
Cucumber, diced	¼	¼
Crisp lettuce, shredded	½	½

First make the sauce filling. Heat the oil in a large saucepan. Add the onion and fry until it is soft. Stir in the meat and fry until it loses its pinkness. Add the sauce and bring to the boil. Reduce the heat to low and simmer for about 40 minutes.

Meanwhile, pour enough oil into a shallow frying-pan to make a 1½cm/¾in layer. When it is hot, carefully arrange one tortilla in the oil and, using tongs, fold over one side, keeping a generous space between the upper and lower sides for the filling. Cook the tortilla in this way, turning it occasionally, until it is crisp throughout. Remove from the oil and keep hot while you make the other tacos in the same way.

To serve the tacos, fill each shell about two-thirds full with the filling and top with the garnishes. Serve at once.

4 Servings

ENCHILADAS
(Stuffed Tortillas with Tomato Sauce)

This is one of the most popular tortilla-based dishes both inside and outside Mexico. Although we have given the classic method of cooking the dish, that is dipping the tortillas in sauce then frying prior to stuffing, this can be rather a messy process and, if you prefer, it would not radically alter the texture of the dish to fry first and dip in sauce later.

	Metric/U.K.	U.S.
Vegetable oil	1 Tbs	1 Tbs
Tortillas	18	18
Salsa de Chile Rojo (red chilli sauce)		

(page 11)	450ml/15oz	2 cups
Grated Parmesan cheese	3 Tbs	3 Tbs
FILLING		
Butter	25g/1oz	2 Tbs
Onion, finely chopped	1	1
Minced (ground) beef	225g/8oz	8oz
Cheddar or jack cheese, grated	50g/2oz	½ cup
Salt and pepper to taste		
Small dried hot red chilli, crumbled	1	1

First prepare the filling. Melt the butter in a frying-pan. Add the onion and fry until it is soft. Stir in the meat and fry until it loses its pinkness. Remove the pan from the heat and transfer the mixture to a bowl. Stir in the remaining filling ingredients until they are thoroughly blended. Set aside.

Preheat the oven to moderate 180°C (Gas Mark 4, 350°F).

Brush a large frying-pan with some of the oil and heat over moderate heat. Holding a tortilla between your finger and thumb, dip it into the chilli sauce, shaking off any excess. Carefully arrange the tortilla in the hot frying-pan and fry for 30 seconds on each side. Using a spatula or tongs, transfer the cooked tortilla to a large plate. Spoon about a tablespoon of filling into the centre, and roll up Swiss (jelly) roll style. Arrange the roll in a large, greased baking dish. Keep hot while you cook and stuff the remaining tortillas in the same way.

When all the tortillas have been stuffed, pour the remaining sauce over them and sprinkle over the grated Parmesan. Put the dish into the oven and bake for 15 to 20 minutes, or until the sauce has browned and is bubbling. Remove from the oven and serve at once.

6 Servings

ENCHILADAS VERDES
(Stuffed Tortillas with Green Tomato Sauce)

The previous recipe is the 'basic' Enchilada recipe, but there are many, many variations on the theme and, in fact, the tortillas may be stuffed with almost anything you fancy— Frijoles Refritos (page 51) and grated or cream cheese, to name only two. This particular recipe

uses cooked chicken in a green tomato sauce, a very popular combination in Mexico.

	Metric/U.K.	U.S.
Vegetable oil	3 Tbs	3 Tbs
Onion, chopped	1	1
Chicken breasts, skinned and boned	3	3
Salsa de Tomatillo Verde (green tomato sauce) (page 11)	725ml/25floz	3 cups
Small dried hot red chillis, crumbled	3	3
Tortillas	12	12
Grated Parmesan cheese	3 Tbs	3 Tbs
Grated Cheddar or jack cheese	3 Tbs	3 Tbs

Heat 2 tablespoons of the oil in a large frying-pan. Add the onion and fry until it is soft. Add the chicken breasts and fry until they are evenly browned. Pour over the sauce, crumble in the chillis and bring to the boil. Reduce the heat to low and simmer for 30 minutes, or until the chicken is cooked through and tender. Remove from the heat and, using a slotted spoon, transfer the chicken to a chopping board. Chop very finely or cut into shreds and set aside.

Preheat the oven to moderate 180°C (Gas Mark 4, 350°F).

Brush a large frying-pan with some of the remaining oil and heat over moderate heat. Holding a tortilla between your finger and thumb, dip it into the green tomato sauce, shaking off any excess. Carefully arrange the tortilla in the hot frying-pan and fry for 30 seconds on each side. Using a spatula or tongs, transfer the cooked tortilla to a large plate. Spoon about 1 tablespoon of shredded chicken into the centre and sprinkle over a little Parmesan cheese. Fold into a neat parcel and arrange the parcel, seam side down, in a large, greased baking dish. Keep hot while you cook and stuff the remaining tortillas in the same way.

When all the tortillas have been stuffed, pour the remaining sauce over them and sprinkle over the grated Cheddar or jack cheese. Put the dish into the oven and bake for 15 to 20 minutes, or until the sauce has browned and is bubbling.

Remove the dish from the oven and serve at once.

4 Servings

Another, more formal variation on tortillas, Enchilladas: tortillas stuffed with a beef mixture then baked in a tomato and cheese sauce.

Meat and Poultry

EMPANADAS
(Meat-Filled Pasties)

These tasty pasties are popular all over Latin America although they originated in Mexico. Picadillo (page 17) can also be used as a filling if you would like a change. Although they are baked in this version, they are also often deep-fried.

Empanadas are small meat-filled pasties popular all over Latin America.

	Metric/U.K.	U.S.
Frozen puff pastry, thawed	425g/14oz	14oz
FILLING		
Butter	25g/1oz	2 Tbs
Medium onion, finely chopped	1	1
Tomatoes, blanched, peeled, seeded and chopped	2	2
Small green pepper, pith and seeds removed and chopped	½	½
Minced (ground) beef	225g/8oz	8oz
Sultanas or seedless raisins	50g/2oz	⅓ cup
Salt and pepper to taste		
Small dried hot red chilli, crumbled	1	1
Ground cumin	½ tsp	½ tsp

To make the filling, melt the butter in a frying-pan. Add the onion, tomatoes and pepper and fry until they are soft. Stir in the meat and fry until it loses its pinkness. Stir in the remaining ingredients and bring to the boil. Reduce the heat to low and cook the mixture for 10 minutes, stirring occasionally. Remove from the heat and set aside.

Preheat the oven to fairly hot 190°C (Gas Mark 5, 375°F).

Roll out the dough on a lightly floured surface into a large square. Using a 13cm/5in pastry cutter, cut the dough into eight circles.

Put about 1 tablespoon of the beef mixture on one side of each circle and fold over the dough to enclose it. Dampen the edges with water and crimp to seal.

Transfer the pasties to a well-greased baking sheet and put the sheet into the oven. Bake for 35 minutes, or until the pastry is cooked and golden brown.

Remove from the oven and serve at once.

4 Servings

PICADILLO
(Minced [Ground] Beef with Apples, Raisins and Olives)

This traditional Mexican dish can be served in any of several ways—by itself with rice for an informal meal or as a filling for tortillas or empanadas (see previous page).

	Metric/U.K.	U.S.
Vegetable oil	3 Tbs	3 Tbs
Large onion, chopped	1	1
Garlic clove, crushed	1	1
Minced (ground) beef	1kg/2lb	2lb
Canned peeled tomatoes	425g/14oz	14oz
Tomato purée (paste)	2 Tbs	2 Tbs
Large cooking apple, peeled, cored and chopped	1	1
Canned Jalapeño chillis, drained and chopped	2	2
Sultanas or seedless raisins	50g/2oz	⅓ cup
Stuffed olives, sliced	10	10
Ground cinnamon	½ tsp	½ tsp
Ground cloves	¼ tsp	¼ tsp
Salt and pepper to taste		
Slivered almonds, toasted	3 Tbs	3 Tbs

Heat the oil in a large saucepan. Add the onion and garlic and fry until they are soft. Stir in the meat and fry until it loses its pinkness. Stir in all the remaining ingredients, except the almonds, and bring to the boil. Reduce the heat to low and simmer for 40 minutes.

Transfer the mixture to a warmed serving dish and scatter over the toasted almonds. Serve at once.

6 Servings

CHILLI CON CARNE I
(Minced [Ground] Beef with Chillis)

This hot, spicy dish could claim dual nationality since tradition has it that it was 'invented' in what are now the border states of the United States and Mexico. Whatever its origins, it remains a popular dish in both the United States and Mexico.

	Metric/U.K.	U.S.
Olive oil	2 Tbs	2 Tbs
Medium onions, finely chopped	2	2
Garlic cloves, crushed	2	2
Minced (ground) beef	700g/1½lb	1½lb
Canned peeled tomatoes	225g/8oz	8oz
Tomato purée (paste)	4 Tbs	4 Tbs
Bay leaf	1	1
Ground cumin	1 tsp	1 tsp
Dried oregano	1 tsp	1 tsp

Chilli con Carne — one of the great classics of Mexican cooking and now enjoyed all over the world.

Calderete al Jerez is a Spanish lamb stew cooked with sherry.

	Metric/U.K.	U.S.
Cayenne pepper	¼ tsp	¼ tsp
Mild chilli powder	1 Tbs	1 Tbs
Salt and pepper to taste		
Beef stock	250ml/8floz	1 cup
Canned red kidney beans, drained	425g/14oz	14oz

Heat the oil in a large saucepan. Add the onions and garlic and fry until they are soft. Stir in the meat and fry until it loses its pinkness. Stir in the tomatoes and can juice, tomato purée (paste), seasonings and stock, and bring to the boil. Reduce the heat to low and cover the pan. Simmer for 1 hour, stirring occasionally.

Stir in the kidney beans, re-cover the pan and simmer for a further 30 minutes. Remove and discard the bay leaf and serve at once.

6 Servings

CHILLI CON CARNE II
(Braising Steak with Chillis)

This fiery variation of Chilli con Carne is the one most popular in Mexico itself. If you prefer a milder taste, seed the chillis before using them, or use mild chilli powder (about 1 to 1½ table-spoons) instead. If you prefer to use milder ancho chillis, use three or four instead of the number indicated below.

	Metric/U.K.	U.S.
Vegetable oil	2 Tbs	2 Tbs
Onion, thinly sliced	1	1
Garlic clove, crushed	1	1
Red pepper, pith and seeds removed and cut into rings	1	1
Small dried hot red chilli, crumbled or canned Jalapeño chilli, drained and chopped	1	1
Braising (chuck) steak, cubed	1kg/2lb	2lb
Salsa de Chile Rojo (red chilli sauce) (page 11)	450ml/15floz	2 cups
Canned red kidney beans, drained	425g/14oz	14oz
Dark brown sugar	25g/1oz	2 Tbs
Salt and pepper to taste		
Finely chopped coriander leaves or parsley	1 Tbs	1 Tbs

Heat the oil in a large saucepan. Add the onion, garlic and pepper and fry until they are soft. Stir in the crumbled or chopped chilli. Add the beef cubes to the pan and fry until they are evenly browned. Stir in all the remaining ingredients, except the coriander or parsley, and bring to the boil. Reduce the heat to low, cover the pan and simmer the stew for 2 hours, or until the meat is cooked through and tender. Uncover for the last 15 minutes of cooking time if you wish to thicken the sauce.

Transfer the mixture to a warmed serving dish and sprinkle over the coriander or parsley. Serve at once.

4–6 Servings

CALDERETA AL JEREZ
(Lamb Stew with Sherry)

	Metric/U.K.	U.S.
Dry sherry	300ml/10floz	1¼ cups
Garlic cloves, crushed	2	2
Boned lamb, cut into cubes	1½kg/3lb	3lb

Salt and pepper to taste		
Ground cumin	1 tsp	1 tsp
Vegetable oil	50ml/2floz	¼ cup
Medium onions, sliced	2	2
Flour	2 Tbs	2 Tbs

Combine the sherry and garlic in a mixing bowl. Add the lamb cubes and baste well. Cover and set aside to marinate at room temperature for 3 hours, basting occasionally. Remove the cubes from the marinade and pat dry with kitchen towels. Reserve the marinade.

Rub the cubes with salt and pepper to taste, then the cumin.

Heat the oil in a large saucepan. Add the lamb and fry until it is evenly browned. Add the onions and fry until they are soft. Stir in the flour until it is well blended, then pour over the reserved marinade, stirring constantly. Bring to the boil. (If the sauce is too thick, add a little water.) Reduce the heat to low, cover the pan and simmer the stew for 1 to 1¼ hours, or until the lamb is cooked through and tender. Remove from the heat and serve at once.

6–8 Servings

CHULETAS DE CORDERO A LA NAVARRA
(Lamb Chops with Ham and Chorizo in Tomato Sauce)

This dish is a speciality of the region of Navarre in the Pyrenees near the French border. Although the ham is traditional to the recipe, it can be omitted if you prefer.

	Metric/U.K.	U.S.
Lamb cutlets	8	8
Salt and pepper to taste		
Olive oil	50ml/2floz	¼ cup
Large onion, chopped	1	1
Garlic cloves, crushed	2	2
Cooked ham, finely chopped	125g/4oz	4oz
Canned peeled tomatoes, chopped	425g/14oz	14oz
Chorizo sausage, thinly sliced	175g/6oz	6oz

Rub the cutlets all over with salt and pepper to taste.

Heat the oil in a large frying-pan. Add the cutlets, a few at a time, and fry until they are evenly browned. Using a slotted spoon or tongs, transfer the cutlets to a baking dish large enough to take them in one layer.

Preheat the oven to moderate 180°C (Gas Mark 4, 350°F).

Add the onion, garlic and ham to the oil remaining in the frying-pan and fry until the onions are soft. Pour over the tomatoes and can juice and bring to the boil, stirring occasionally. Stir in seasoning to taste. Pour the mixture over the lamb cutlets and put the baking dish into the oven. Bake for 20 minutes.

Remove from the oven and arrange the sausage slices over the mixture. Return the dish to the oven for a further 15 minutes, or until the cutlets are cooked through and tender.

Remove from the oven and serve at once.

4 Servings

Tinga de Cerdo y Ternera is a Mexican speciality of pork and veal cubes cooked in a sauce of green tomatoes.

TINGA DE CERDO Y TERNERA
(Pork and Veal Stew with Green Tomatoes)

This Mexican stew incorporates one of the specialities of the country, green tomatoes.

	Metric/U.K.	U.S.
Butter	50g/2oz	4 Tbs
Vegetable oil	2 Tbs	2 Tbs
Pork, cubed	1kg/2lb	2lb
Lean veal, cubed	1kg/2lb	2lb
Onions, finely chopped	2	2
Garlic cloves, crushed	3	3
Green tomatoes, blanched, peeled and chopped	1kg/2lb	2lb
Green peppers, pith and seeds removed and chopped	3	3
California green chillis, chopped	4	4
Tomato purée (paste)	2 Tbs	2 Tbs
Chopped fresh marjoram	1 Tbs	1 Tbs
Chopped chives	1 Tbs	1 Tbs
Chopped fresh basil	1 Tbs	1 Tbs
Grated nutmeg	2 tsp	2 tsp
Salt and pepper to taste		
Sugar	1 tsp	1 tsp
Chicken stock	250ml/8floz	1 cup
Dry sherry	250ml/8floz	1 cup
Double (heavy) cream	75ml/3floz	$\frac{3}{8}$ cup

Melt the butter with the oil in a large flameproof casserole. Add the meat and fry until it is evenly browned. Transfer to a plate. Add the onions and garlic to the casserole and fry until they are soft. Stir in the tomatoes, peppers, chillis, tomato purée (paste), herbs, seasoning and sugar and cook for 5 minutes, stirring constantly.

Return the meat to the casserole and pour over the stock and sherry. Bring to the boil. Reduce the heat to low, cover the casserole and simmer the stew for 1½ hours, or until the meat is cooked through and tender.

Remove from the heat and stir in the cream. Serve at once, straight from the casserole.

8–10 Servings

ARROZ CON CERDO
(Mexican Rice and Pork)

	Metric/U.K.	U.S.
Vegetable oil	2 Tbs	2 Tbs
Medium onion, chopped	1	1
Minced (ground) pork	½kg/1lb	1lb
Sausagemeat	225g/8oz	8oz
Celery stalks, cut into 2½cm/1in pieces	2	2
Small green pepper, pith and seeds removed and cut into rings	1	1
Sultanas or seedless raisins	75g/3oz	½ cup
Garlic clove, crushed	1	1
Ground cumin	½ tsp	½ tsp
Small dried hot red chilli, crumbled	1	1
Salt and pepper to taste		
Long-grain rice, soaked in cold water for 30 minutes and drained	175g/6oz	1 cup
Canned peeled tomatoes	425g/14oz	14oz
Water	125ml/4floz	½ cup
Tomato purée (paste)	2 Tbs	2 Tbs
Juice of ½ lemon		
Pine nuts	3 Tbs	3 Tbs

Preheat the oven to moderate 180°C (Gas Mark 4, 350°F).

Heat the oil in a flameproof casserole. Add the onion and fry until it is soft. Stir in the pork and sausagemeat and fry until they lose their pinkness. Stir in the vegetables, sultanas or raisins, garlic, cumin, chilli, seasoning and rice and fry for 5 minutes, stirring constantly. Stir in the tomatoes and can juice, water and tomato purée (paste) and bring to the boil. Reduce the heat to low, cover the casserole and simmer for 10 minutes. Transfer the casserole to the oven and bake for 25 minutes.

Remove the casserole from the oven and sprinkle the lemon juice and pine nuts over the top. Return to the oven and bake, uncovered, for a further 10 minutes.

Remove from the oven and serve at once, straight from the casserole.

4–6 Servings

Arroz con Cerdo is a Mexican dish of pork and rice.

LOMO DE CERDO CON VINO BLANCO
(Loin of Pork with White Wine Sauce)

	Metric/U.K.	U.S.
Boned loin of pork, rolled	1 × 1kg/2lb	1 × 2lb
Garlic cloves, crushed	3	3
Salt and pepper to taste		
Olive oil	3 Tbs	3 Tbs
Onions, sliced	2	2
Dry white wine	300ml/10floz	1¼ cups
Bouquets garnis	2	2
Cornflour (cornstarch), blended with 3 Tbs water	1 Tbs	1 Tbs

Rub the pork all over with the garlic and salt and pepper to taste, and set aside for 30 minutes.

Heat the oil in a flameproof casserole or large saucepan. Add the pork and fry until it is evenly browned. Add the onions and fry until they are soft. Pour over the wine and add the bouquets garnis. Bring to the boil, reduce the heat to low and cover the casserole. Simmer for 2¼ hours, or until the pork is cooked through and tender.

Transfer the pork to a warmed serving dish and keep hot. Bring the pan liquid to the boil, stirring constantly. Add the cornflour (cornstarch) mixture and cook, stirring constantly, for 2 minutes, or until the sauce thickens and is smooth.

Pour a little of the sauce over the pork and transfer the rest to a warmed sauceboat. Serve at once, with the meat.

4–6 Servings

COCHINILLO ASADO
(Roast Suckling Pig)

This is one of the great specialities of Castile, and of Segovia in particular. Stuffings vary from cook to cook, but almost any fairly light one would be suitable instead of the ingredients suggested below. The pig should be roasted for about 20 minutes per half kilo (pound).

Suckling pig is one of the great festive dishes of Spain, and particularly of the province of Castile. In Cochinillo Asado the pig has been stuffed with garlic, onions and herbs, but if you prefer, any stuffing of your choice may be used.

	Metric/U.K.	U.S.
Garlic cloves, crushed	3	3

Onions, chopped	2	2
Bouquets garnis	2	2
Chopped parsley	1 bunch	1 bunch
Suckling pig, prepared	1 × 7¼kg/16lb	1 × 16lb
Salt and pepper to taste		
Olive oil	50ml/2floz	¼ cup
Lemon juice	125ml/4floz	½ cup
GARNISH		
Small red apple	1	1
Fresh herbs to taste		
Large oranges, sliced	4	4
Black grapes, seeded and halved	125g/4oz	1 cup

Put the garlic, onions, bouquets garnis and parsley into the pig and close the cavity with skewers or a trussing needle and thread. Rub the pig all over with salt and pepper. Then rub over half the olive oil and lemon juice. Set aside for 1 hour, then rub the remaining oil and juice into the skin of the pig, using your fingertips.

Preheat the oven to hot 220°C (Gas Mark 7, 425°F).

Place a small piece of wood or a ball of aluminium foil in the mouth of the pig to wedge it open, and place balls of foil in the eye sockets. Cover the ears with foil and curl the tail and secure it with a wooden cocktail stick. Pull the front legs forwards and the back legs forwards and tie them with string.

Transfer the pig, on its stomach, to a deep roasting pan and place the pan in the oven. Roast for 30 minutes. Reduce the oven temperature to warm 170°C (Gas Mark 3, 325°F) and roast the pig for a further 5½ to 6 hours, basting frequently with the pan juices. Drain off the cooking juices occasionally, leaving about a 1cm/½in depth.

Increase the oven temperature to hot 220°C (Gas Mark 7, 425°F) and roast the pig for a final 20 minutes, or until the skin is crisp. Remove from the oven.

To serve the pig, untie the legs and remove the wood or foil from the mouth, eye socket and ears. Untie the tail. Transfer the pig to a large serving platter and surround with the garnishes. Insert the apple into the pig's mouth if you wish, or you can cut it into slices and arrange with the orange.

Serve at once.

14–16 Servings

TERNERA AL JEREZ
(Veal Escalopes with Olives and Sherry)

This festive dish features two of Spain's most popular products—olive oil and sherry, together with one of her favourite meats, veal.

	Metric/U.K.	U.S.
Olive oil	75ml/3floz	⅜ cup
Shallots, chopped	3	3
Garlic cloves, crushed	3	3
Small green pepper, pith and seeds removed and chopped	1	1
Button mushrooms, sliced	125g/4oz	1 cup
Tomatoes, blanched, peeled and chopped	3	3
Lean smoked ham, chopped	50g/2oz	2oz
Green olives, stoned (pitted) and blanched	8	8
Veal escalopes, pounded until thin	4	4
Seasoned flour (flour with salt and pepper to taste)	50g/2oz	½ cup
Dry sherry	50ml/2floz	¼ cup
Water	50ml/2floz	¼ cup

Heat half the oil in a frying-pan. Add the shallots, garlic and green pepper and fry until they are soft. Add the mushrooms, tomatoes, ham and olives and cook for 20 minutes, stirring occasionally, until the mixture has thickened.

Coat the escalopes in the seasoned flour, shaking off any excess.

Heat the remaining oil in a large, deep casserole. Add the escalopes and cook for 3 to 4 minutes on each side, or until they are cooked through and tender. Using tongs, transfer the veal to a plate.

Pour the sherry and water into the casserole and bring to the boil. Stir in the tomato mixture and return the escalopes to the casserole, basting them with the mixture. Reduce the heat to low, cover the casserole and simmer for 5 minutes.

Transfer the mixture to a warmed serving dish and serve at once.

4 Servings

TERNERA A LA VALENCIANA
(Spanish Veal Escalopes with Orange and Sherry Sauce)

	Metric/U.K.	U.S.
Veal escalopes, pounded thin	4	4
Salt and pepper to taste		
Lean smoked ham	4 slices	4 slices
Olive oil	50ml/2floz	¼ cup
Onion, sliced	1	1
Grated orange rind	1 tsp	1 tsp
Orange juice	175ml/6floz	¾ cup
Dry sherry	125ml/4floz	½ cup
Cornflour (cornstarch), blended with 2 Tbs water	2 tsp	2 tsp

Rub the escalopes with salt and pepper. Lay the ham slices over the escalopes, trimming to fit if necessary. Roll up Swiss (jelly) roll style, securing with wooden cocktail sticks or thread.

Heat the oil in a large frying-pan. Add the rolls and fry until they are evenly browned. Using a slotted spoon, transfer the rolls to a plate.

Add the onion to the pan and fry until it is soft. Stir in the orange rind, juice and sherry and bring to the boil. Reduce the heat to low and return the rolls to the pan. Simmer for 15 to 20 minutes, turning the rolls in the sauce occasionally, or until the meat is cooked through and tender.

Transfer the rolls to a warmed serving dish and keep hot while you finish the sauce.

Stir the cornflour (cornstarch) mixture into the pan liquid and cook, stirring constantly, until it thickens and is smooth. Pour over the rolls and serve at once.

4 Servings

RINONES AL JEREZ
(Kidneys in Sherry Sauce)

	Metric/U.K.	U.S.
Olive oil	50ml/2floz	¼ cup
Lambs' kidneys, cleaned, prepared and chopped into small pieces	16	16
Salt and pepper to taste		
Small onion, finely chopped	1	1
Garlic cloves, crushed	2	2
Flour	1 Tbs	1 Tbs
Chicken stock	125ml/4floz	½ cup
Dry sherry	125ml/4floz	½ cup

Heat half the oil in a frying-pan. Add the kidneys and seasoning and fry until they are cooked through and tender. Using a slotted spoon, transfer the pieces to a plate. Keep warm.

Add the onion and garlic to the pan and fry until they are soft. Remove from the heat and keep hot.

Sherry not unnaturally is used extensively in Spanish cooking and nowhere more successfully than in this dish of lambs' kidneys, Rinones al Jerez. Served, as in the picture, on a bed of saffron rice it makes a delightful and colourful main dish.

Heat the remaining oil in a small saucepan. Remove the pan from the heat and stir in the flour to form a smooth paste. Gradually add the stock, stirring constantly. Return the pan to the heat and bring to the boil, stirring constantly. Cook for 2 minutes, stirring constantly, or until the sauce is smooth and thick. Stir in the reserved onion and garlic, reduce the heat to low and simmer for 3 minutes. Remove the pan from the heat.

Return the frying-pan to the heat, add the sherry and bring to the boil. Add the kidneys and onion sauce and bring to the boil, stirring constantly. Reduce the heat to low and simmer for a further 5 minutes.

Transfer the mixture to a warmed serving dish and serve at once.

4 Servings

JAMON CON NABOS
(Spanish Ham and Turnip Stew)

Serrano ham is the traditional ingredient for this warming Spanish stew, but if it is not available any other smoked ham or, in fact, any cooked ham, may be substituted.

	Metric/U.K.	U.S.
Vegetable oil	50ml/2floz	¼ cup
Onion, chopped	1	1
Garlic clove, chopped	1	1
Serrano ham, coarsely chopped	½kg/1lb	1lb
Flour	1 Tbs	1 Tbs
Water	600ml/1 pint	2½ cups
Salt and pepper to taste		
Bay leaf	1	1
Chopped parsley	1 Tbs	1 Tbs
Turnips, diced	½kg/1lb	1lb

Heat the oil in a large saucepan. Add the onion and garlic and fry until they are soft. Add the ham and fry for a further 5 minutes, stirring frequently. Stir in the flour until it forms a smooth paste. Fry for 2 minutes, stirring constantly.

Add all of the remaining ingredients and bring to the boil. Reduce the heat to low, cover the pan and simmer for 1½ hours, or until the turnips are cooked and tender.

Transfer the mixture to a warmed serving

dish. Remove and discard the bay leaf and serve at once.

4–6 Servings

FABADA ASTURIANA
(Bean and Sausage Stew)

This classic dish is one of the national dishes of the province of Asturias in northwestern Spain and is a cross between a soup and a stew. The traditional alubia beans are sometimes difficult to obtain outside Spain and haricot (dried white) beans may be substituted.

	Metric/U.K.	U.S.
Water	1¾l/3 pints	7½ cups
Dried white alubia beans, soaked overnight in cold water and drained	225g/8oz	1⅓ cups
Dried broad (fava or lima) beans, soaked overnight in cold water and drained	225g/8oz	1⅓ cups
Large onion, chopped	1	1
Garlic cloves, crushed	2	2
Morcilla or blood sausage, sliced	125g/4oz	4oz
Dried oregano	1 tsp	1 tsp
Small chorizo sausages, sliced	2	2
Bacon, chopped	2 slices	2 slices
Serrano ham, chopped	50g/2oz	2oz
Ground saffron	½ tsp	½ tsp
Salt and pepper to taste		

Pour the water into a large saucepan and bring to the boil. Add the alubia and broad (fava or lima) beans, onion and garlic and bring back to the boil. Reduce the heat to low, cover the pan and simmer for 45 minutes to 1 hour, or until the beans are cooked and tender.

Add the morcilla or blood sausage, oregano, chorizo sausages, bacon, ham, saffron and seasoning and stir to mix. Simmer for a further 30 minutes.

Transfer the mixture to a warmed serving bowl and serve at once.

6–8 Servings

Fadaba Asturiana comes from northwestern Spain and is one of several Spanish classics that could correctly be described as a cross between a soup and a stew — in either case it is fabulous to eat and practically a meal in itself.

CALLOS VIZCAINOS
(Tripe in Wine Sauce)

	Metric/U.K.	U.S.
Chicken stock	300ml/10floz	1¼ cups
Dry white wine	300ml/10floz	1¼ cups
Dried thyme	½ tsp	½ tsp
Bay leaf	1	1
Medium onions, 1 left whole and 2 finely chopped	3	3
Tripe, blanched, and cut into strips about 5cm/2 in long	1kg/2lb	2lb
Tomatoes, blanched, peeled, seeded and chopped	4	4
Tomato purée (paste)	2 Tbs	2 Tbs
Celery stalk, chopped	1	1
Salt and pepper to taste		

Put the stock, wine, herbs, whole onion and tripe into a large saucepan and bring to the boil. Reduce the heat to low and simmer slowly for about 1 hour, or until the tripe is cooked through and tender. Using a slotted spoon, transfer the tripe to a plate and keep hot.

Add the tomatoes, tomato purée (paste), celery and chopped onions to the liquid and simmer for a further 30 minutes. Remove from the heat and strain the mixture into a bowl. Remove and discard the bay leaf. Mash the vegetables with the back of a wooden spoon to extract all the juices.

Return the tripe and strained sauce to the pan and season to taste. Simmer gently for 20 minutes. Remove from the heat, transfer to a warmed serving dish.

Serve at once.

4 Servings

OLLA PODRIDA
(Meat and Vegetable Stew)

This filling Spanish dish predates the Inquisition and was, in fact, originally Jewish. It was altered during the Inquisition by the Jewish community to include pork to convince the skeptical (and particularly their Inquisitors!) of their commitment to Christianity.

	Metric/U.K.	U.S.
Dried chick-peas, soaked in cold water overnight and drained	½kg/1lb	2⅔ cups
Large onions, sliced	2	2
Garlic cloves, crushed	2	2
Bouquet garni	1	1
Boned shoulder butt or leg of pork, cubed	½kg/1lb	1lb
Bacon, cubed	½kg/1lb	1lb
Stewing (chuck) beef, cubed	225g/8oz	8oz
Small boiling chicken, cut into serving pieces	1 × 2kg/4lb	1 × 4lb
Salt and pepper to taste		
Leeks, white part only, thinly sliced	2	2
Large carrots, thinly sliced	2	2
Cabbage, shredded	1	1
Large potatoes, cubed	2	2
Tomatoes, blanched, peeled and chopped	4	4
Chorizo sausage, sliced	1	1
Chopped parsley	2 Tbs	2 Tbs

Put the chick-peas in a large saucepan and pour over just enough cold water to cover. Set the pan over moderate heat and bring to the boil. Reduce the heat to low and simmer for 2 to 2½ hours or until the chick-peas are very tender, skimming off any scum that rises to the surface with a slotted spoon.

Add the onions, garlic, bouquet garni, meat, chicken pieces and seasoning. Add more cold water so that the meats are almost covered. Bring back to the boil, skimming off any scum that rises to the surface. Reduce the heat to low and simmer for 2 hours, or until all the meats are cooked through and tender. Remove from the heat and transfer to a large bowl. Set aside in a cool place until a layer of fat forms on top. Skim off and discard the fat.

Return the mixture to the saucepan and stir in the vegetables and sausage. Return to moderate heat and cook for 30 minutes, or until the vegetables are cooked and tender.

Transfer the stew to a large serving bowl. Sprinkle over the parsley and serve at once.

8–10 Servings

POLLO A LA ESPANOLA
(Spanish Chicken)

	Metric/U.K.	U.S.
Olive oil	50ml/2floz	¼ cup
Chicken, cut into 8 serving pieces	1 × 2kg/4lb	1 × 4lb
Medium onions, thinly sliced	2	2
Garlic cloves, crushed	1	1
Large red pepper, pith and seeds removed and chopped	1	1
Canned artichoke hearts, drained	425g/14oz	14oz
Chicken stock	450ml/15floz	2 cups
Salt and pepper to taste		
Cayenne pepper	¼ tsp	¼ tsp
Saffron threads, soaked in 1 Tbs water	½ tsp	½ tsp
Stuffed olives, halved	16	16
Beurre manié (one part butter and two parts flour blended)	25g/1oz	2 Tbs

Pollo a la Espanola is a simple chicken stew enlivened with stuffed olives and saffron.

Preheat the oven to moderate 180°C (Gas Mark 4, 350°F).

Heat the oil in a large, deep frying-pan. Add the chicken pieces and fry until they are evenly browned. Using tongs, transfer the pieces, as they brown, to a large flameproof casserole.

Add the onions, garlic and pepper to the pan and fry until they are soft. Add the artichoke hearts and fry for a further 2 minutes. Pour over the stock and stir in the seasoning, cayenne and saffron mixture. Bring to the boil, stirring occasionally. Pour the mixture over the chicken pieces.

Put the casserole into the oven and cook for 1 hour, or until the chicken pieces are cooked through and tender. Remove from the oven and transfer the chicken pieces to a

warmed serving dish. Keep hot while you finish the sauce.

Add the olives to the casserole and place over moderate heat. Bring to the boil, stirring occasionally. Stir in the beurre manié, a little at a time, until the sauce has thickened and is smooth.

Pour the sauce over the chicken pieces and serve at once.

4 Servings

ARROZ CON POLLO
(Chicken with Saffron Rice)

	Metric/U.K.	U.S.
Vegetable oil	3 Tbs	3 Tbs
Streaky (fatty) bacon, chopped	6 slices	6 slices
Chicken, cut into serving pieces	1 × 2½kg/5lb	1 × 5lb
Seasoned flour (flour with salt and pepper to taste)	40g/1½oz	⅓ cup
Onions, chopped	2	2
Garlic clove, crushed	1	1
Canned peeled tomatoes	425g/14oz	14oz
Canned pimientos, drained	75g/3oz	3oz
Paprika	2 tsp	2 tsp
Ground saffron	¼ tsp	¼ tsp
Salt	1 tsp	1 tsp
Water	600ml/1 pint	2½ cups
Long-grain rice, soaked in cold water for 30 minutes and drained	225g/8oz	1⅓ cups
Frozen peas, thawed	175g/6oz	1 cup

Heat the oil in a flameproof casserole. Add the bacon and fry until it is crisp and has rendered its fat. Transfer the bacon to kitchen towels to drain.

Coat the chicken pieces in the seasoned flour, shaking off any excess. Add the pieces to the casserole and fry until they are evenly browned. Using tongs, transfer the pieces to a plate.

Preheat the oven to moderate 180°C (Gas Mark 4, 350°F).

Drain off most of the oil from the casserole and add the onions and garlic. Fry until they

are soft. Arrange the chicken pieces over the onions and add the tomatoes and can juice, the pimientos, paprika, saffron, salt and water. Bring to the boil, then stir in the rice. Cover the casserole and put into the oven. Cook for 35 minutes. Stir in the peas and bacon and cook for a further 15 to 20 minutes, or until the chicken pieces are cooked through and tender.

Remove the casserole from the oven and serve at once.

4–6 Servings

POLLO AL CHILINDRON
(Chicken with Peppers and Tomatoes)

This is a popular dish from Aragon in Spain. Lamb and pork are also often cooked in this way.

	Metric/U.K.	U.S.
Chicken, cut into serving pieces	1 × 2kg/4lb	1 × 4lb
Seasoned flour (flour with salt and pepper to taste)	40g/1½oz	⅓ cup
Olive oil	50ml/2floz	¼ cup
Large onion, chopped	1	1
Garlic cloves, crushed	2	2
Large red peppers, pith and seeds removed and chopped (or 425g/14oz canned pimientos, drained and chopped)	2	2
Serrano ham, chopped	50g/2oz	2oz
Canned peeled tomatoes	425g/14oz	14oz
Saffron threads, soaked in 2 Tbs water	½ tsp	½ tsp
Cayenne pepper	¼ tsp	¼ tsp
Salt and pepper to taste		

Coat the chicken pieces in the seasoned flour, shaking off any excess.

Heat the oil in a large, heavy-based saucepan. Add the chicken pieces and fry until they are evenly browned. Using tongs, transfer to a plate.

Add the onion, garlic and red peppers and fry until they are soft. Stir in the ham, tomatoes and can juice, saffron mixture, cayenne and seasoning and bring to the boil. Return the chicken pieces to the pan and

Arroz con Pollo was originally Spanish but is now just as popular in Mexico — one of the kinder legacies of the conquest. It is a mixture of chicken pieces, saffron rice, bacon and peas.

reduce the heat to low. Cover and simmer for
1 hour, or until the chicken pieces are cooked
through and tender.

4–6 Servings

POLLO RELLENO
(Stuffed Chicken, Andalusian-Style)

	Metric/U.K.	U.S.
Chicken	1 × 2kg/4lb	1 × 4lb
Butter	50g/2oz	4 Tbs
Olive oil	1 Tbs	1 Tbs
Large onion	1	1
Bouquet garni	1	1
Flour	1 Tbs	1 Tbs
Tomato purée (paste)	2 Tbs	2 Tbs
Salt and pepper to taste		
Dry white wine	125ml/4floz	½ cup
STUFFING Cooked rice	125g/4oz	2 cups
Cooked ham, diced	125g/4oz	4oz
Paprika	2 tsp	2 tsp
Salt	1 tsp	1 tsp
GARNISH Vegetable oil	2 Tbs	2 Tbs
Large onion, thinly sliced into rings	1	1
Green peppers, pith and seeds removed and sliced into rings	2	2
Tomatoes, blanched, peeled and chopped	½kg/1lb	1lb
Salt and pepper to taste		

Rub the chicken inside and out with kitchen
towels. Mix all of the stuffing ingredients
together and spoon into the cavity. Close
the cavity with a skewer or a trussing needle
and thread.

Melt the butter with the oil in a large,
heavy-based saucepan. Add the chicken and
fry until it is evenly browned. Add the onion
and bouquet garni and reduce the heat to
low. Cover and simmer the chicken for about
1 to 1¼ hours, or until it is cooked through and
tender.

Meanwhile, to make the garnish, heat the
oil in a large frying-pan. Add the onion and
fry until it is soft. Add all of the remaining
ingredients and cook gently until they are
soft. Remove from the heat and keep hot.

Remove the chicken from the pan and
arrange it on a large, warmed serving dish.
Discard the onion and bouquet garni. Bring
the pan juices to the boil, then sprinkle over
the flour, stirring constantly. Stir in the
tomato purée (paste), seasoning and wine and
bring to the boil. Cook, stirring constantly,
for 2 to 3 minutes, or until the sauce thickens
and is smooth.

Arrange the garnish around the chicken,
then pour over the sauce. Serve at once.

4 Servings

EMPANADA GALLEGA
(Chicken and Ham Pie)

*Empanadas in Mexico are small turnover-like
pasties, but in Spain they are usually more
substantial, large pies that can constitute a
main dish. Galicia is particularly famous for
its empanadas and small empanadas called
empanadillas, and they can have a variety of
fillings—pork is very popular as are fresh
sardines. The filling below is another popular
one, of chicken and ham.*

	Metric/U.K.	U.S.
PASTRY Flour	450g/1lb	4 cups
Salt	1 tsp	1 tsp
Ground cloves	¼ tsp	¼ tsp
Olive oil	75ml/3floz	⅜ cup
Cold water	175ml/6floz	¾ cup
Egg white, beaten with 2 Tbs milk	1	1
FILLING Chicken, cut into serving pieces	1 × 1½kg/3lb	1 × 3lb
Onion, quartered	1	1
Bouquet garni	1	1
Peppercorns	1 tsp	1 tsp
Olive oil	50ml/2floz	¼ cup
Leek, white part only, chopped	1	1
Garlic cloves, crushed	2	2
Green pepper, pith and seeds removed and		

finely chopped	1	1
Serrano ham, chopped	125g/4oz	4oz
Tomatoes, blanched, peeled, seeded and chopped	4	4

First make the filling. Put the chicken into a large saucepan and just cover with water or stock. Add the onion, bouquet garni and peppercorns and bring to the boil, skimming off any scum which rises to the surface. Reduce the heat to low, cover the pan and simmer the chicken for 1 hour, or until it is cooked through and tender. Remove the chicken from the pan and set aside until it is cool enough to handle. Discard the cooking liquid and flavourings.

Meanwhile, to make the pastry, sift the flour, salt and cloves into a large bowl. Make a well in the centre and pour over the oil and water. Gradually incorporate the flour into the liquid, beating until it comes away from the sides of the bowl. Turn the dough out on to a lightly floured surface and knead lightly until it is smooth and elastic. Cover with a damp cloth and set aside in the refrigerator for 30 minutes.

Cut the chicken into bite-sized pieces and discard any bones or skin.

Heat the oil in a large, deep frying-pan. Add the leek, garlic and pepper and fry until

A classic stuffed chicken dish from Andalusia in southern Spain, Pollo Relleno.

A Spanish dish of partridges cooked in white wine with vegetables, Perdices Estofadas.

they are soft. Stir in the ham, tomatoes and chicken and cook for 5 minutes, stirring constantly. Remove the pan from the heat.

Preheat the oven to moderately hot 190°C (Gas Mark 5, 375°F).

Divide the dough in half. On the lightly floured surface, roll out each half to a 23cm/9in circle. Carefully transfer one half to a well-greased baking sheet. Arrange the filling in the centre of the circle, leaving at least a a 2½cm/1in edge all the way round. Using a rolling pin, carefully arrange the second dough circle over the filling. Roll up the edges and crimp them to seal. Cut a deep slit in the centre of the top dough circle. Brush the top and sides of the dough with the egg white mixture and put the baking sheet into the oven. Bake for 30 to 40 minutes, or until the pie is golden brown.

Remove from the oven and transfer the pie to a warmed serving dish. Serve at once.

6 Servings

MOLE POBLANO
(Turkey with Chocolate Sauce)

This could almost be described as the Mexican national dish and legend has it that it was invented by the nuns of a convent in honour of a visiting bishop—from scraps they had in a rather bare kitchen plus a turkey in the yard. The sauce traditionally is supposed to have thirty ingredients in it, although it is now usually simplified to more manageable proportions, as here.

	Metric/U.K.	U.S.
Turkey, cut into serving pieces	1 × 4½kg/10lb	1 × 10lb
Seasoned flour (flour with salt and pepper to taste)	125g/4oz	1 cup
Lard or butter	75g/3oz	6 Tbs
Salt	1 tsp	1 tsp
Bouquets garnis	2	2
SAUCE		
Large onion, finely chopped	1	1
Garlic clove, crushed	1	1
Sultanas or seedless raisins	75g/3oz	½ cup
Ground almonds	125g/4oz	1 cup
Tomatoes, blanched,		

peeled, seeded and chopped	3	3
Sesame seeds, toasted	4 Tbs	4 Tbs
Tortillas, crumbled	2	2
Aniseed	½ tsp	½ tsp
Ground cinnamon	½ tsp	½ tsp
Ground cloves	½ tsp	½ tsp
Ground coriander	½ tsp	½ tsp
Salt and pepper to taste		
Small dried hot red chillis, crumbled	3	3
Jalapeño chilli, chopped	1	1
Turkey stock (made from the giblets, etc)	600ml/1 pint	2½ cups
Dark cooking (semi-sweet) chocolate, crumbled	50g/2oz	2 squares

Coat the turkey pieces in the seasoned flour, shaking off any excess.

Melt half the lard or butter in a large, heavy-based saucepan. Add the turkey pieces and fry until they are deeply and evenly browned. Add enough water just to cover the pieces, then add the salt and bouquets garnis. Bring to the boil. Reduce the heat to low, cover the pan and simmer the turkey for 1½ hours, or until the pieces are cooked through and tender. Remove from the heat, drain the turkey pieces and set them aside.

Meanwhile, to make the sauce, melt the remaining fat in a large saucepan. Add the onion and garlic and fry until they are soft. Stir in the sultanas or raisins, almonds, tomatoes, half the sesame seeds, the tortillas, spices, seasoning and chillis and cook for 8 minutes, stirring occasionally. Add half the stock and bring to the boil. Remove from the heat.

Add the remaining stock and blend the mixture, a little at a time, in a blender until it forms a smooth purée. Return the purée to the saucepan. Add the chocolate and simmer gently, stirring constantly, until it melts and the sauce has thickened and is smooth.

Arrange the turkey pieces in a large serving dish and pour over a little of the sauce. Garnish with the remaining sesame seeds. Pour the remaining sauce into a warmed sauceboat and serve at once, with the turkey pieces.

8–10 Servings

PERDICES ESTOFADAS
(Partridges with White Wine and Vegetables)

	Metric/U.K.	U.S.
Partridges, trussed and larded	4	4
Salt and pepper to taste		
Butter	50g/2oz	4 Tbs
Lean bacon, chopped	4 slices	4 slices
Dry white wine	125ml/4floz	½ cup
Water	250ml/8floz	1 cup
Garlic cloves, crushed	3	3
Bouquet garni	1	1
Grated nutmeg	¼ tsp	¼ tsp
Grated lemon rind	2 tsp	2 tsp
Small onions, blanched	12	12
Small new potatoes, scraped	12	12
Small carrots, cut into quarters, lengthways	6	6
Green peas, weighed after shelling	50g/2oz	⅓ cup
Small courgettes (zucchini), sliced	4	4

Sprinkle the partridges with salt and pepper to taste.

Melt the butter in a flameproof casserole or large, heavy-based saucepan. Add the partridges and fry until they are evenly browned. Using tongs, transfer them to a plate and keep hot.

Add the bacon to the casserole and fry until it is crisp and has rendered its fat. Transfer the bacon to kitchen towels to drain. Pour off most of the cooking fat from the casserole.

Pour the wine and water into the casserole, then add the garlic, bouquet garni, nutmeg and lemon rind. Return the partridges to the casserole and bring the liquid to the boil. Stir in the onions, potatoes and carrots and reduce the heat to low. Simmer the mixture for 15 minutes. Add the remaining ingredients and reserved bacon and cook for a further 15 minutes, or until the partridges are cooked through and tender.

Remove from the heat and remove and discard the bouquet garni. Remove the trussing thread and lard.

Serve at once.

4 Servings

Fish and Seafood

MERO A LA NARANJA
(Fish with Orange Sauce)

The mero is a Mediterranean fish and is very popular in Spain. Halibut or grouper may be substituted if it is unavailable.

Mero is a Mediterranean fish and not always available outside that part of the world, but this delightful fish with orange sauce can be made with halibut or even cod or whiting if mero is not available.

	Metric/U.K.	U.S.
Mero steaks	6	6
Butter	50g/2oz	4 Tbs
Flour	2 Tbs	2 Tbs
Chicken stock	250ml/8floz	1 cup
Orange juice	150ml/5floz	⅝ cup
Salt and pepper to taste		
Orange, thinly sliced	1	1

Preheat the grill (broiler) to high.

Arrange the fish steaks in the lined grill (broiler) pan. Cut half the butter into small pieces and dot over and around the fish. Place the pan under the grill (broiler) and grill (broil) for 3 to 5 minutes on each side. Using tongs, transfer the fish steaks to a large, warmed serving dish. Keep hot while you prepare the sauce.

Melt the remaining butter in a small saucepan. Remove from the heat and stir in the flour to form a smooth paste. Gradually stir in the stock, orange juice and seasoning and return the pan to low heat. Bring to the boil, stirring constantly. Cook for 2 to 3 minutes, stirring constantly, or until the sauce is thick and smooth.

Pour the sauce over the fish and garnish with the orange slices.

Serve at once.

6 Servings

MERLUZA A LA MARINERA
(Hake Fillets in Tomato and Almond Sauce)

If hake is unavailable, cod fillets may be substituted in this Spanish dish.

	Metric/U.K.	U.S.
Olive oil	3 Tbs	3 Tbs
Small onion, chopped	1	1
Garlic cloves, crushed	2	2
Ground almonds	50g/2oz	½ cup
Fresh breadcrumbs	15g/½oz	¼ cup
Chopped parsley	4 Tbs	4 Tbs
Tomatoes, blanched, peeled, seeded and chopped	½kg/1lb	1lb
Hake fillets	1kg/2lb	2lb
Hot water	1¼l/2 pints	5 cups
Juice of ½ lemon		
Salt	½ tsp	½ tsp
Bouquet garni	1	1
Flaked almonds	2 Tbs	2 Tbs

Heat the oil in a large frying-pan. Add the onion and garlic and fry until they are soft. Remove the pan from the heat and stir in the ground almonds, breadcrumbs, 3 tablespoons of parsley and the tomatoes. Return to the heat and cook for 5 minutes, or until the liquid has evaporated and the mixture is thick. Remove from the heat and set aside.

Preheat the oven to moderate 180°C (Gas Mark 4, 350°F).

Arrange the fish fillets, in one layer, in a large baking pan. Pour over the hot water and lemon juice and add the salt and bouquet garni. Cover with foil and place the tin in the oven. Poach for 8 to 12 minutes, or until the flesh flakes easily. Remove from the oven and transfer the fillets to a warmed serving dish. Keep hot while you prepare the sauce.

Strain and reserve 75ml/3floz (⅜ cup) of the cooking liquid. Add it to the tomato and almond mixture in the frying-pan and stir well to blend. Set the pan over moderate heat and cook until the mixture is smooth, stirring constantly.

Pour the sauce over the fish and sprinkle over the flaked almonds and remaining parsley. Serve at once.

6 Servings

MERLUZA A LA GALLEGA
(Hake with Potatoes)

This classic dish is from Galicia, a province of Spain noted for the excellence of its fish. If hake is unobtainable, cod may be substituted.

	Metric/U.K.	U.S.
Potatoes	6	6
Olive oil	75ml/3floz	⅜ cup
Onion, chopped	1	1
Garlic cloves, crushed	2	2
Fish stock	1¼l/2 pints	5 cups
Hake fillets, skinned and halved	700g/1½lb	1½lb
Wine vinegar	1 Tbs	1 Tbs
Cayenne pepper	1 tsp	1 tsp

Parboil the potatoes in salted water for 5 minutes. Drain and set aside until they are cool enough to handle. Cut them into thick rounds.

Heat the oil in a large, deep frying-pan. Add the onion and garlic and fry until they are soft. Add the potato rounds and fry gently until they are evenly browned. Pour over 300ml/10floz (1¼ cups) of the fish stock and bring to the boil. Reduce the heat to low and simmer the mixture for 20 minutes.

Meanwhile, arrange the fish fillets in a shallow saucepan and pour over the remaining stock. Poach the fish over gentle heat for about 15 minutes, or until the flesh flakes easily. Drain and discard the stock.

Mix the vinegar and cayenne together and carefully stir into the potato mixture. Simmer for 1 minute. Remove from the heat and transfer the potato mixture to a shallow, warmed serving dish. Arrange the fish fillets on top and serve at once.

6 Servings

MERLUZA KOSKERA
(Hake with Clams and Asparagus)

	Metric/U.K.	U.S.
Clams, scrubbed	16	16
Hake or cod steaks	4	4
Seasoned flour (flour with salt and pepper to taste)	50g/2oz	½ cup
Olive oil	50ml/2floz	¼ cup
Garlic cloves, crushed	3	3
Chopped parsley	2 Tbs	2 Tbs

Dry white wine	150ml/5floz	⅝ cup
Frozen peas, thawed	125g/4oz	⅔ cup
Frozen asparagus tips, thawed and trimmed to uniform length	8	8
Hard-boiled eggs, halved lengthways	2	2

Half-fill a large saucepan with water and bring to the boil. Add the clams, cover and cook for 6 to 8 minutes, or until the shells open (discard any clams that do not open). Drain and reserve about 125ml/4floz (½ cup) of the liquid. Set the clams aside, discard the shells and keep hot.

Coat the fish steaks in the seasoned flour, shaking off any excess. Heat the oil in a large, deep frying-pan. Add the garlic and fry for 1 minute, stirring constantly. Add the fish steaks and fry until they are evenly browned. Add the parsley, wine and reserved clam liquid and bring to the boil. Reduce the heat to low and cover the pan. Simmer for 10 minutes, or until the flesh flakes easily.

Stir in the peas, asparagus tips and reserved clams. Simmer for a further 3 minutes, or until they are heated through.

Transfer the mixture to a warmed serving dish, arranging the vegetables, clams and sauce decoratively over and around the fish. Garnish each fish steak with a hard-boiled egg half and serve at once.

4 Servings

BESUGO AL HORNO
(Baked Bream with Potatoes)

	Metric/U.K.	U.S.
Bream, each cleaned but with the head and tails left on	2 × 1kg/2lb	2 × 2lb
Salt	1½ tsp	1½ tsp
Lemon, cut into 6 sections	1	1
Small black olives	2	2
Fresh breadcrumbs	25g/1oz	½ cup
Garlic cloves, crushed	2	2
Paprika	1 Tbs	1 Tbs
Chopped parsley	1 Tbs	1 Tbs

Medium potatoes, cut into ½cm/¼in rounds	3	3
Black pepper	½ tsp	½ tsp
Water	250ml/8floz	1 cup
Olive oil	75ml/3floz	⅜ cup

Preheat the oven to moderate 180°C (Gas Mark 4, 350°F).

Wash and dry the fish on kitchen towels. Sprinkle over 1 teaspoon of salt and make three parallel, crosswise, cuts across each fish—they should be about 1cm/½in deep, about 7½cm/3in long and about 4cm/1½in apart. Insert a section of lemon, skin side up, into each cut and insert an olive in the eye socket of each fish.

Mix together the breadcrumbs, garlic, paprika and parsley. Spread the potato rounds evenly on the bottom of a large, shallow baking pan and sprinkle over the remaining salt and the pepper. Pour the water over the potatoes. Place the fish on top of the potatoes, then brush them all over with the oil. Sprinkle over the breadcrumb mixture.

Put the pan into the oven and bake for 30 minutes, or until the fish flesh flakes easily. Remove from the oven and serve at once.

4 Servings

CEVICHE
(Mackerel Fillets Marinated in Lemon Juice)

This traditional Mexican dish is now popular all over Central and South America, with slight variations from country to country. Originally limes were used, but since they can be difficult to obtain, fresh lemon juice is suggested instead. If you prefer to use limes, however, use 250ml/8floz (1 cup) of lime juice and 250ml/8floz (1 cup) of lemon juice, instead of the amount suggested below.

	Metric/U.K.	U.S.
Fresh lemon juice	450ml/15floz	2 cups
Dried small hot red chilli, crumbled	1	1
Large onions, thinly sliced into rings	2	2
Garlic clove, chopped	½	½
Salt and pepper to taste		

Escabeche is a Mediterranean dish of pickled cooked fish.

Large mackerels, filleted and cut into 2½cm/1in pieces	3	3
Large sweet potatoes, unpeeled	3	3
Crisp lettuces, separated into leaves and chilled	2	2
Fresh sweetcorn, outer husks and thread removed and cut crosswise into 5cm/2in rounds	4	4
Fresh red chilli, split, seeded and cut into thin pieces	1	1

Combine the lemon juice, dried chilli, onion rings, garlic and seasoning in a large pitcher.

Arrange the fish pieces in a shallow porcelain dish and pour the lemon juice over them. (Add more lemon juice if the mixture does not completely cover the fish pieces.) Cover the dish and transfer it to the refrigerator. Leave for at least 3 hours, or until it is opaque and white.

About 30 minutes before serving time, bring 1¾l/3 pints (7½ cups) of water to the boil in a large saucepan. Put the sweet potatoes into the pan and cover. Reduce the heat to moderate and cook for 30 to 35 minutes, or until they are cooked through and tender.

While the potatoes are cooking, arrange a bed of lettuce leaves on individual serving plates.

Remove the pan from the heat and drain the potatoes. Peel and cut each one into three slices. Keep hot while you cook the sweetcorn.

Pour 1¼l/2 pints (5 cups) of water into a saucepan and bring to the boil. Drop the corn rounds into the pan and boil for 4 to 5 minutes or until they turn bright yellow. Remove from the heat and drain the corn.

Remove the marinated fish from the refrigerator and divide it equally between the plates. Garnish with the onion rings and strips of fresh chilli pepper. Arrange the sweet potato slices and corn rounds around the fish and serve at once.

4 Servings

ESCABECHE
(Pickled Fish)

This Spanish (and Provençal) dish is probably the ancestor of the Mexican Ceviche and is used extensively throughout the Mediterranean countries to preserve fish when it is plentiful and cheap. Any type of fish fillet may be used, such as mackerel, cod, halibut or haddock, or even whole small fish such as red mullet.

	Metric/U.K.	U.S.
Flour	3 Tbs	3 Tbs
Salt	1½ tsp	1½ tsp
White fish fillets	700g–1kg/ 1½lb–2lb	1½–2lb
Olive oil	150ml/5floz	⅝ cup
Large onions, sliced	2	2
Red pepper, pith and seeds removed and cut into strips	1	1
Garlic cloves, chopped	2	2
Fresh red chilli, chopped	1	1
Bay leaves	3	3
Black peppercorns	¼ tsp	¼ tsp
Red wine vinegar	300ml/10floz	1¼ cups

Combine the flour and 1 teaspoon of salt on a plate. Coat the fish pieces in the flour, shaking off any excess.

Heat 75ml/3floz (⅜ cup) of oil in a large frying-pan. Add the fish and fry for 4 to 5 minutes on each side, or until they are golden brown and flake easily. Transfer the fish to kitchen towels to drain.

Pour off the oil and rinse out the pan. Pour the remaining oil into the pan and heat. Add the onions and fry until they are soft. Stir in the pepper, garlic, chilli, bay leaves, remaining salt, the peppercorns and vinegar and bring to the boil. Cook for 2 minutes.

Arrange the fish in an earthenware or heat-proof glass dish. Pour the mixture over the fish and cover the dish with a lid or foil. Allow to cool to room temperature, then transfer the dish to the refrigerator. Leave to marinate for 2 to 3 days. Serve straight from the dish.

4 Servings

HUACHINANGO VERACRUZANO
(Red Snapper, VeraCruz Style)

If red snapper is not available, gurnet or sea bream may be substituted.

	Metric/U.K.	U.S.
Vegetable oil	50ml/2floz	¼ cup
Large onion, chopped	1	1
Garlic clove, crushed	1	1
Canned peeled tomatoes	700g/1½lb	1½lb
Small dried hot red chillis, crumbled, or Jalapeño chillis, drained and chopped	2	2
Stuffed green olives, chopped	6	6
Black olives, stoned (pitted), and chopped	4	4
Red snapper fillets	700g/1½lb	1½lb
Seasoned flour (flour with salt and pepper to taste)	40g/1½oz	⅓ cup
Butter	50g/2oz	4 Tbs

Heat the oil in a large saucepan. Add the onion and garlic and fry until they are soft. Purée the tomatoes and can juice in a blender until they are soft (or push them through a food mill) and stir them into the onion mixture with the chillis and olives. Bring to the boil, reduce the heat to low and simmer the sauce for 20 minutes.

Meanwhile, coat the fillets in the seasoned flour, shaking off any excess.

Melt the butter in a large frying-pan. Add the fillets and fry for 4 to 6 minutes on each side or until they are evenly browned and the flesh flakes easily.

Another Latin American favourite which originated in Mexico, Ceviche is fillets of mackerel marinated in lemon or lime juice.

Transfer the fish to a warmed serving dish. Pour over the sauce and serve at once.

4 Servings

HUACHINANGO YUCATECO
(Red Snapper, Yucatan Style)

If red snapper is not available, gurnet or sea bream may be substituted.

	Metric/U.K.	U.S.
Butter	50g/2oz	4 Tbs
Medium onion, chopped	1	1
Garlic clove, crushed	1	1
Small red pepper, pith and seeds removed and chopped	1	1
Small green pepper, pith and seeds removed and chopped	1	1
Chopped coriander leaves	1 Tbs	1 Tbs
Ground cumin	1 tsp	1 tsp
Orange juice	125ml/4floz	½ cup
Grated orange rind	½ tsp	½ tsp
Salt and pepper to taste		
Red snapper, cleaned but with the head and tail left on	1 × 2½kg/5lb	1 × 5lb
Black or green olives, stoned (pitted) and chopped	6	6
Avocado, stoned (pitted) and thinly sliced	1	1

Melt half the butter in a frying-pan. Add the onion, garlic and peppers and fry until they are soft. Stir in the coriander, cumin, orange juice, orange rind and seasoning and bring to the boil. Simmer for 2 minutes, then remove the pan from the heat. Set aside.

Preheat the oven to moderate 180°C (Gas Mark 4, 350°F).

Cut the remaining butter into small dice and scatter it over the bottom of a large, shallow casserole dish. Arrange the fish on top and pour over the orange juice mixture. Scatter over the olives. Put the dish into the oven and bake for 25 to 30 minutes, or until the fish flesh flakes easily, basting the fish from time to time with the sauce mixture.

Remove from the heat and garnish with the avocado slices. Serve at once.

6 Servings

SALMONETES ANDALUZA
(Red Mullet, Andalusian Style)

	Metric/U.K.	U.S.
Red mullets, cleaned and with the eyes removed	6	6
Juice of 1 lemon		
Ground pine nuts	75g/3oz	¾ cup
Garlic cloves, crushed	2	2
Small onion, finely chopped	1	1
Chopped parsley	4 Tbs	4 Tbs
Salt and pepper to taste		
Olive oil	3 Tbs	3 Tbs
Green pepper, pith and seeds removed and cut into ½cm/¼in strips	1	1
Medium tomatoes, blanched, peeled, seeded and sliced	6	6
Butter, cut into small pieces	25g/1oz	2 Tbs
Black olives	6	6

Put the mullets in a large shallow bowl and pour over the lemon juice. Set aside at room temperature for 15 minutes.

Preheat the oven to moderate 180°C (Gas Mark 4, 350°F).

Combine the pine nuts, garlic, onion, parsley and seasoning and gradually beat in the oil until the mixture is smooth and blended. Set aside.

Remove the fish from the marinade, discarding the marinating liquid and pat dry with kitchen towels. Arrange the fish, in one layer, in a large baking dish. Spread over the pine nut mixture making sure that each fish is evenly covered. Arrange the pepper strips over the fish and cover with the tomatoes. Dot over the butter and place the dish in the oven. Bake for 25 minutes, or until the fish flesh flakes easily.

Remove the dish from the oven and transfer the fish to a warmed serving dish. Place the

olives in the uppermost eye socket of each fish and serve at once.

6 Servings

MARMITAKO
(Tuna Steaks with Potatoes)

This delicious dish is a classic from the Basque country, bordering on France. If tuna steaks are not available, substitute halibut or cod instead.

	Metric/U.K.	U.S.
Olive oil	125ml/4floz	½ cup
Onions, chopped	2	2
Garlic clove, crushed	1	1
Medium potatoes, sliced into 1cm/½in thick rounds	3	3
Small red peppers, pith and seeds removed and cut into strips	2	2
Salt and pepper to taste		
Paprika	1½ tsp	1½ tsp
Tuna fish steaks, about 2½ cm/1in thick	4	4
Water	175ml/6floz	¾ cup

Heat the oil in a large, deep frying-pan. Add the onions and garlic and fry until they are soft. Add the potatoes and peppers and fry for 5 minutes, turning occasionally. Stir in the seasoning and paprika. Add the tuna steaks and fry until they are lightly browned on both sides. Pour over the water and bring to the boil.

Salmonetes Andaluzá — red mullets marinated in an oil and pine nut mixture then baked with pepper and tomatoes.

Reduce the heat to low, cover the pan and simmer for 15 minutes, or until the fish flesh flakes easily.

Remove the pan from the heat and transfer the mixture to a warmed serving dish. Serve at once.

4 Servings

BACALAO A LA VISCAINA
(Salt Cod, Biscay Style)

Salt cod is immensely popular all over Spain and it is cooked in a variety of delicious ways. This particular dish is a classic from the Basque country.

	Metric/U.K.	U.S.
Salt cod, soaked in cold water for 24 hours	1kg/2lb	2lb
Seasoned flour (flour with salt and pepper to taste)	40g/1½oz	⅓ cup
Olive oil	50ml/2floz	¼ cup
Large onions, chopped	2	2
Garlic cloves, crushed	2	2
Canned peeled tomatoes	700g/1½lb	1½lb
White bread, crusts removed	2 slices	2 slices
Fresh red or green chillis, seeded and chopped	2	2

Estofado de Anguila — Spanish Eel Stew.

44

	Metric/U.K.	U.S.
Canned pimientos, drained and cut into strips	425g/14oz	14oz
Fine dry breadcrumbs	3 Tbs	3 Tbs
Finely chopped parsley	1 Tbs	1 Tbs

Drain the salt cod and transfer to a large saucepan. Just cover with cold water. Set the pan over low heat and bring to the boil. Remove the pan from the heat and drain the salt cod. When it is cool enough to handle, remove the skin and bones and cut into 5cm/2in pieces. Coat the fish pieces in the seasoned flour, shaking off any excess and set aside.

Heat half the oil in a large, deep frying-pan. Add the onions and garlic and fry until they are soft. Add the tomatoes and can juice and reduce the heat to low. Simmer for 5 minutes.

Meanwhile, heat 1 tablespoon of the remaining oil in a small saucepan. Add the bread slices and fry until they are evenly browned. Remove from the heat and cut the bread into small pieces. Stir the bread pieces and chillis into the tomato mixture and simmer for a further 10 minutes.

Preheat the oven to moderate 180°C (Gas Mark 4, 350°F).

Spread half the tomato mixture over the bottom of a medium baking dish. Cover with the salt cod pieces, then top with the remaining tomato mixture. Arrange the pimiento strips over the top.

Mix the breadcrumbs and parsley together and sprinkle over the mixture, then pour over the remaining oil. Put the dish into the oven and cook for 15 to 20 minutes, or until the topping is browned.

Remove from the heat and serve at once.

6 Servings

ESTOFADO DE ANGUILA
(Eel Stew)

	Metric/U.K.	U.S.
Olive oil	3 Tbs	3 Tbs
Chopped blanched almonds	50g/2oz	½ cup
Large red pepper, pith and seeds removed and chopped	1	1
Large onion, sliced	1	1
Garlic cloves, crushed	3	3
Black pepper	¼ tsp	¼ tsp
Dried thyme	¼ tsp	¼ tsp
Paprika	1 tsp	1 tsp
Cayenne pepper	½ tsp	½ tsp
Eels, skinned and cut into serving pieces	1kg/2lb	2lb
Fish stock	900ml/1½ pints	3¾ cups
Cornflour (cornstarch), blended with 1 Tbs water	1 tsp	1 tsp

Heat the oil in a large, heavy-based saucepan. Add the almonds, pepper, onion and garlic and fry until the almonds are golden brown and the onion is soft. Add the pepper, thyme, paprika and cayenne and cook for 2 minutes, stirring constantly. Add the eel pieces and cook, turning them frequently, for 5 minutes. Pour over the fish stock and bring to the boil. Reduce the heat to low, cover the pan and simmer the mixture for 30 minutes.

Stir in the cornflour (cornstarch) mixture and simmer for 2 to 3 minutes, stirring constantly, until the sauce thickens and is smooth.

Remove the pan from the heat and serve at once.

6 Servings

CALAMARES EN SU TINTA
(Squid in its own Ink)

	Metric/U.K.	U.S.
Olive oil	75ml/3floz	⅜ cup
Squid, cleaned thoroughly and cut into 1cm/½in pieces (ink sacs reserved)	1½kg/3lb	3lb
Medium onion, finely chopped	1	1
Garlic cloves, crushed	2	2
Chopped parsley	1 Tbs	1 Tbs
Ground mace	⅛ tsp	⅛ tsp
Salt and pepper to taste		
Cold water	250ml/8floz	1 cup
Flour	2 Tbs	2 Tbs

Heat the oil in a large saucepan. Add the squid, onion, garlic and parsley and fry until they are lightly browned. Add the mace and seasoning and reduce the heat to low. Cover and simmer for 20 minutes.

Meanwhile, mash the ink sacs through a strainer set over a bowl to extract the ink. Pour over the water and mash again. Using a whisk, beat in the flour until the ink and water mixture is smooth.

Pour the sauce over the squid mixture and bring to the boil, stirring constantly. Reduce the heat to very low, cover and simmer for 5 minutes, stirring occasionally. Remove the pan from the heat and set aside, covered, for 5 minutes.

Transfer the mixture to a large, warmed serving dish.

Serve at once.

4–6 Servings

ALMEJAS A LA MARINERA
(Clams in Tomato and Garlic Sauce)

	Metric/U.K.	U.S.
Olive oil	3 Tbs	3 Tbs
Large onion, chopped	I	I
Garlic cloves, crushed	2	2
Fresh white breadcrumbs	40g/1½oz	¾ cup
Tomatoes, blanched, peeled, seeded and chopped	700g/1½lb	1½lb
Hard-boiled egg yolks, strained	2	2
Salt and pepper to taste		
Small clams, scrubbed	48	48
Dry white wine	450ml/15floz	2 cups
Chopped parsley	2 Tbs	2 Tbs
Hard-boiled egg whites, finely chopped	2	2
Lemons, cut into wedges	2	2

Heat the oil in a frying-pan. Add the onion and garlic and fry until they are soft. Add the breadcrumbs, tomatoes, egg yolks and seasoning and cook, stirring constantly, until the mixture forms a thick purée. Remove from the heat and set aside.

Put the clams into a large, heavy-based saucepan and pour over the wine. Bring to the boil, then reduce the heat to low. Cover the pan and steam the clams for 6 to 8 minutes, or until the shells open (discard any clams that do not open).

Transfer the clams to a large, warmed serving bowl. Strain the liquid from the pan and add to the tomato purée. Pour the sauce over the clams. Garnish with the parsley and egg whites and serve at once, accompanied by the lemon wedges.

4 Servings

PAELLA I
(Chicken and Seafood with Rice)

Paella is probably the single most famous dish from Spain and it is one of those dishes whose origins were modest and simple but which is now both rich and ornate to make. Almost any ingredient can be added or subtracted but saffron-flavoured rice is traditional as are the chicken and shrimps.

	Metric/U.K.	U.S.
Cooked lobster, shell split, claws cracked and grey sac removed	1 × 700g/1½lb	1 × 1½lb
Olive oil	2 Tbs	2 Tbs
Chicken, cut into serving pieces	1 × 1kg/2lb	1 × 2lb
Chorizo sausage, sliced	I	I
Medium onion, sliced	I	I
Garlic clove, crushed	I	I
Tomatoes, blanched, peeled, seeded and chopped	3	3
Large red pepper, pith and seeds removed and chopped	I	I
Salt and pepper to taste		
Paprika	I tsp	I tsp
Long-grain rice, soaked in cold water for 30 minutes and drained	350g/12oz	2 cups
Water	600ml/1 pint	2½ cups
Juice of 1 lemon		
Saffron threads, soaked in 125ml/4floz water	¼ tsp	¼ tsp

	Metric/U.K.	U.S.
Green peas, weighed after shelling	225g/8oz	1⅓ cups
Large prawns or shrimps, shelled	175g/6oz	6oz
Mussels, scrubbed, steamed for 6 to 8 minutes	20	20
Chopped parsley	1 Tbs	1 Tbs

Remove the lobster meat from the shell and claws and cut it into 2½cm/1in pieces. Set aside.

Heat the oil in a large, deep frying-pan. Add the chicken and chorizo and fry until the chicken is deeply and evenly browned. Using tongs, remove the chicken pieces and chorizo from the pan. Set aside and keep hot.

Add the onion and garlic to the pan and fry until they are soft. Add the tomatoes, pepper, seasoning and paprika and cook for 10 to 12 minutes, stirring occasionally, or until the mixture is thick.

Add the rice to the pan and, shaking the pan frequently, fry it for 3 minutes, or until it is transparent. Add the water, lemon juice and saffron mixture and bring to the boil. Reduce the heat to low and stir in the peas. Return the chicken and sausage to the pan and cook for 15 minutes, stirring occasionally. Add the lobster meat, prawns or shrimps and mussels and cook for a further 5 minutes, or until the chicken is cooked through and tender, and the cooking liquid has been absorbed.

Remove the pan from the heat. Sprinkle over the parsley and serve at once.

6 Servings

PAELLA II
(Chicken and Seafood with Rice)

This is a slightly more modest version of this Spanish favourite.

	Metric/U.K.	U.S.
Cooked lobster, shell split, claws cracked and grey sac removed	1 × 700g/1½lb	1 × 1½lb
Olive oil	75ml/3floz	⅜ cup
Chicken, cut into serving pieces	1 × 1½kg/3lb	1 × 3lb

Lean bacon, chopped	6 slices	6 slices
Large tomatoes, blanched, peeled, seeded and chopped	2	2
Garlic cloves, crushed	2	2
Mange-tout or green beans, cut into lengths	225g/8oz	2 cups
Long-grain rice, soaked in cold water for 30 minutes and drained	450g/1lb	2⅔ cups
Paprika	2 tsp	2 tsp
Water	1¼l/2 pints	5 cups
Salt	2 tsp	2 tsp
Ground saffron	¼ tsp	¼ tsp
Small clams, scrubbed and steamed for 6 to 8 minutes, and with one shell removed	12	12
Snails	6	6
Baby squid, cleaned thoroughly and chopped	225g/8oz	8oz
Lemon wedges	6	6

Remove the lobster meat from the shell and claws and cut it into 2½cm/1in pieces. Set aside.

Heat the oil in a large, deep frying-pan. Add the chicken pieces and bacon and fry until the chicken is deeply and evenly browned. Add the tomatoes, garlic and mange-tout or beans and fry for a further 5 minutes, stirring occasionally. Using a slotted spoon, transfer the mixture to a bowl. Set aside and keep hot.

Add the rice and paprika to the pan and cook for 3 minutes, stirring frequently, or until the rice is translucent. Add the water, salt and saffron and bring to the boil, stirring constantly. Reduce the heat to low and return the chicken and vegetable mixture to the pan. Cook for 10 minutes, stirring occasionally. Add the clams, snails, squid and lobster and cook for a further 5 to 10 minutes, or until the chicken is cooked through and tender and the cooking liquid has been absorbed.

Garnish with lemon wedges and serve.

6 Servings

ZARZUELA
(Fish Stew)

A frothy Catalan sea-food stew.

	Metric/U.K.	U.S.
Olive oil	150ml/5floz	⅝ cup
Large onion, sliced	I	I
Squid, cleaned thoroughly and cut into rings (sac removed)	225g/8oz	8oz
Tomatoes, blanched, peeled and chopped	6	6
Chopped fresh basil	2 tsp	2 tsp
Dry white wine	125ml/4floz	½ cup
Eel, cut into 2½cm/1in pieces	350g/12oz	12oz
Clams, scrubbed and steamed for 6 to 8 minutes	24	24
Salt and pepper to taste		
Fish stock	300ml/10floz	1¼ cups
Canned tuna fish, drained and flaked	200g/7oz	7oz
Sole fillets, skinned and cut into 2½cm/1in pieces	255g/8oz	8oz
Ground almonds	50g/2oz	½ cup
Chopped parsley	2 Tbs	2 Tbs
Ground saffron	½ tsp	½ tsp
Garlic cloves, crushed	2	2
White bread, fried in olive oil and quartered	2 slices	2 slices
Cooked prawns or shrimps, unpeeled	225g/8oz	8oz

Heat all but 1 tablespoon of the oil in a large saucepan. Add the onion and fry until it is golden brown. Add the squid, tomatoes, basil and wine and cook for 3 minutes, stirring occasionally. Add the eel, clams, salt, pepper and stock, reduce the heat to low and simmer for 10 minutes. Add the tuna fish and sole and simmer for a further 10 minutes.

Meanwhile, put the almonds, parsley, saffron, garlic, the remaining oil and one piece of bread into a mortar. Add 1 tablespoon of liquid from the fish mixture and pound the mixture with a pestle until it forms a paste.

Spread the paste on the bottom of a warmed serving dish. Remove the pan from the heat and pour the fish mixture into the serving dish. Garnish with the remaining fried bread and the prawns or shrimps.

Serve at once.

6 Servings

Zarzuela means operetta in Spanish, and the name of this frothy concoction of mixed seafood becomes all the more appropriate when you taste it.

Vegetables and Eggs

JUDIAS VERDES CON SALSA DE TOMATE
(Green Beans in Tomato Sauce)

Torrijas de Maiz Tierno — deep-fried sweetcorn fritters.

	Metric/U.K.	U.S.
Butter	25g/1oz	2 Tbs
Garlic cloves, crushed	2	2
Green or French beans, cut into 2½cm/1in lengths	1kg/2lb	5⅓ cups
Canned peeled tomatoes, chopped	700g/1½lb	1½lb
Finely chopped chives	1 Tbs	1 Tbs
Salt and pepper to taste		
Bay leaf	1	1
Chopped pine nuts	1 Tbs	1 Tbs
Lemon juice	1 Tbs	1 Tbs

Melt the butter in a large saucepan. Add the garlic and fry for 2 minutes, stirring constantly. Add the beans and cook for 4 minutes, stirring occasionally. Stir in the tomatoes and can juice, and all the remaining ingredients and bring to the boil, stirring constantly. Reduce the heat to low and simmer for 25 to 30 minutes or until the beans are very tender and the liquid has reduced a little.

Remove and discard the bay leaf. Transfer the mixture to a warmed serving dish and serve at once.

6 Servings

TORRIJAS DE MAIZ TIERNO
(Corn Fritters)

	Metric/U.K.	U.S.
Sweetcorn kernels	225g/8oz	1⅓ cups
Flour	50g/2oz	½ cup
Sugar	2 Tbs	2 Tbs
Salt and pepper to taste		
Eggs, lightly beaten	2	2
Grated Parmesan cheese	2 Tbs	2 Tbs
Sufficient vegetable oil for deep-frying		

Combine the sweetcorn, flour, sugar, seasoning, eggs and cheese until they are thoroughly blended. Set aside.

Fill a large deep-frying pan one-third full with oil and heat until it reaches 185°C (360°F) on a deep-fat thermometer, or until a small cube of stale bread dropped into the oil turns golden brown in 50 seconds. Carefully lower a few tablespoons of the sweetcorn mixture into the oil and fry for 3 to 4 minutes,

or until the fritters are golden brown. Using a slotted spoon, transfer the fritters to kitchen towels to drain. Keep hot while you cook the remaining mixture in the same way.

Transfer the fritters to a warmed serving dish and serve at once.

4 Servings

GARBANZOS A LA MEXICANA
(Spicy Chick-Peas)

	Metric/U.K.	U.S.
Dried chick-peas, soaked overnight in cold water and drained	275g/10oz	1⅔ cups
Salt	1½ tsp	1½ tsp
Streaky (fatty) bacon, diced	6 slices	6 slices
Large onion, roughly chopped	1	1
Garlic clove, crushed	1	1
Small red pepper, pith and seeds removed and chopped	1	1
Black pepper	¼ tsp	¼ tsp
Small dried hot red chilli, crumbled	1	1
Dried oregano	½ tsp	½ tsp
Canned tomato sauce (not ketchup)	150g/5oz	5oz

Put the chick-peas and 1 teaspoon of salt into a saucepan and pour over enough water just to cover. Set over moderately high heat and bring to the boil. Reduce the heat to low and simmer for 1 hour, or until the chick-peas are cooked and tender. Drain the chick-peas and set aside.

Fry the bacon in a medium, heavy-based saucepan until it is crisp and has rendered all of its fat. Add the onion, garlic and pepper and fry until they are soft. Stir in the remaining salt, the pepper, chilli, oregano, tomato sauce and chick-peas. Bring to the boil and reduce the heat to low. Simmer for 10 minutes, stirring occasionally.

Transfer the mixture to a warmed serving dish and serve at once.

4 Servings

FRIJOLES REFRITOS
(Refried Beans)

This is one of the staple foods of Mexico and can be used in a variety of ways—as an accompaniment to meat, as a filling for tortillas or, as here, with the addition of sausage and cheese, as a filling meal on its own.

Frijoles Refritos (refried beans) is one of the staples of Mexico and is used as a snack, with the addition of sausages and cheese as a meal in itself, or as a filling for tortillas or empanadas.

	Metric/U.K.	U.S.
Dried kidney or pinto beans, soaked in cold water overnight and drained	225g/8oz	1⅓ cups
Salt	1 tsp	1 tsp
Small chorizo sausage, skinned and diced	1	1
Lard or vegetable fat	3 Tbs	3 Tbs
Onion, chopped	1	1
Medium tomatoes, blanched, peeled, seeded and chopped	3	3

Zapellitos Rellenos are courgettes (zucchini) stuffed with a mixture of cheese, breadcrumbs, garlic and basil.

Small dried hot red chillis, crumbled	2	2
Cheddar or jack cheese, grated	50g/2oz	½ cup

Put the beans and ½ teaspoon of salt into a saucepan and pour over enough water just to cover. Set over moderately high heat and bring to the boil. Reduce the heat to low, cover the pan and simmer for 1½ hours, or until the beans are cooked and tender. Drain the beans and purée them in a blender. Set aside.

Meanwhile, fry the chorizo in a small frying-pan for 5 minutes, stirring occasionally. Do not add any fat as the sausage will let out a good deal of its own. Using a slotted spoon, transfer the chorizo pieces to kitchen towels to drain. Set aside.

Melt the lard or fat in a large frying-pan. Add the onion and fry until it is soft. Stir in the tomatoes, remaining salt and chilli and cook, stirring frequently, for 5 minutes, or until the mixture becomes pulpy. Stir in the sausage, the puréed beans and the cheese and cook, stirring and turning frequently, for 10 minutes or until the cheese has melted.

Transfer the mixture to a warmed serving dish and serve at once.

4 Servings

ZAPELLITOS RELLENOS
(Stuffed Courgettes [Zucchini] Mexican Style)

	Metric/U.K.	U.S.
Courgettes (zucchini)	6	6
Garlic clove, crushed	1	1
Dry breadcrumbs	125g/4oz	$1\frac{1}{3}$ cups
Chopped fresh basil	1 Tbs	1 Tbs
Fontina, Cheddar or jack cheese, grated	175g/6oz	$1\frac{1}{2}$ cups
Salt and pepper to taste		
Eggs, lightly beaten	2	2
Butter, melted	50g/2oz	4 Tbs

Cut the courgettes (zucchini) in half lengthways and carefully hollow out the flesh to within $\frac{1}{2}$cm/$\frac{1}{4}$in of the skin. Set the shells aside.

Chop the flesh, then press with the back of a wooden spoon to extract as much juice as possible and drain it away. Set the flesh aside.

Preheat the oven to fairly hot 200°C (Gas Mark 6, 400°F).

Combine the courgette (zucchini) flesh, garlic, breadcrumbs, basil, cheese, seasoning, eggs and half the melted butter until they are thoroughly blended.

Arrange the courgette (zucchini) shells, skin side down, in a well-greased shallow baking dish. Stuff with the breadcrumb mixture and pour over the remaining melted butter. Put the dish into the oven and bake for 20 to 30 minutes, or until the top is brown and bubbling.

Remove the dish from the oven and serve at once.

6 Servings

COLACHE
(Courgettes [Zucchini], Sweetcorn and Tomatoes)

	Metric/U.K.	U.S.
Butter or lard	40g/1½oz	3 Tbs
Courgettes (zucchini), sliced crosswise	4	4
Onion, chopped	1	1
Garlic, crushed	1	1
Green pepper, pith and seeds removed and chopped	1	1
Medium tomatoes, blanched, peeled and chopped	2	2
Small dried hot red chilli, chopped	1	1
Water	125ml/4floz	½ cup
Sweetcorn kernels	175g/6oz	1 cup
Salt and pepper to taste		

Melt the butter or lard in a saucepan. Add the courgette (zucchini) slices and fry until they are evenly browned. Add the onion, garlic and pepper and fry until they are soft. Stir in the tomatoes, chilli and water and bring to the boil, stirring occasionally. Reduce the heat to low and simmer for 10 minutes.

Stir in the sweetcorn and seasoning and simmer for a further 5 to 10 minutes, or until the courgettes (zucchini) are cooked and tender.

Transfer the mixture to a warmed serving dish and serve at once.

4–6 Servings

PISTO MANCHEGO
(Mixed Vegetable Stew)

This dish is a variation on the Basque pipérade filling and variations of it are cooked all over northern Spain. Ham is sometimes added to the vegetables and with its addition, the dish becomes a light main dish rather than a filling accompaniment.

	Metric/U.K.	U.S.
Olive oil	50ml/2floz	¼ cup
Onions, chopped	2	2
Courgettes (zucchini), sliced crosswise	4	4
Large green pepper, pith and seeds removed and chopped	1	1
Large red pepper, pith and seeds removed and chopped	1	1
Canned peeled tomatoes	425g/14oz	14oz
Paprika	1½ tsp	1½ tsp
Salt and pepper to taste		
Eggs, lightly beaten	2	2

Heat the oil in a shallow saucepan. Add the onions, courgettes (zucchini) and peppers and fry until they are soft. Purée the tomatoes and can juice in a blender and stir into the vegetable mixture. Bring to the boil, reduce the heat to low and simmer the mixture, stirring occasionally, for 35 minutes, or until the vegetables are cooked and tender.

Combine the paprika, seasoning and eggs until they are thoroughly blended. Stir into the vegetable mixture and stir and beat until the eggs have scrambled.

Transfer the mixture to a warmed serving dish and serve at once.

4 Servings

CHILES RELLENOS I
(Stuffed Green Chillis)

Green, California-type chillis are often stuffed in Mexico, and with a variety of different materials. Picadillo (page 17) for instance, Frijoles Refritos (page 51), or, as here, simple sticks of cheese. The sauce is traditional to the dish but can be omitted if you prefer.

	Metric/U.K.	U.S.
Canned California green chillis	2 × 200g/7oz	2 × 7oz
Cheddar or jack cheese, cut into strips short enough to fit into the chillis	175g/6oz	6oz
Seasoned flour (flour with salt and pepper to taste)	50g/2oz	½ cup
Sufficient vegetable oil for deep-frying		
Salsa de Chile Rojo (red chilli sauce) (page 11)	300ml/10floz	1¼ cups
COATING		
Eggs, separated	3	3
Water	1 Tbs	1 Tbs
Cornflour (cornstarch)	3 Tbs	3 Tbs

Drain the chillis and gently cut a slit halfway down the side of each one. Remove any seeds and membrane and rinse under cold running water. Insert the cheese piece, then coat in the seasoned flour, shaking off any excess.

To make the coating, beat the yolks, water and cornflour (cornstarch) together until

they are well blended. Beat the egg whites until they form stiff peaks. Fold into the egg yolk mixture.

Fill a large saucepan one-third full with oil and heat until it reaches 185°C (360°F) on a deep-fat thermometer, or until a small cube of stale bread dropped into the oil turns golden in 50 seconds. Dip the chillis in the batter to coat them thoroughly and place them one by one in the hot oil (use a saucer to slide them in if necessary). Fry for 3 to 4 minutes, or until the coating is puffed up and lightly browned. Remove from the oil and drain on kitchen towels.

Transfer the cooked chillis to a warmed serving dish and pour over the sauce. Serve at once.

4 Servings

CHILES RELLENOS II
(Stuffed Peppers, Yucatan Style)

	Metric/U.K.	U.S.
Large green or red peppers	4	4
Olive oil	50ml/2floz	¼ cup
Medium onions, diced	2	2
Garlic cloves, crushed	2	2
Dried small hot red chillis, crumbled	2	2
Minced (ground) beef	½kg/1lb	1lb
Dried oregano	1 tsp	1 tsp
Salt	1 tsp	1 tsp
Bay leaves	2	2
Tabasco sauce	½ tsp	½ tsp
Flour	2 Tbs	2 Tbs
Beef stock	250ml/8floz	1 cup
Tomato purée (paste)	3 Tbs	3 Tbs
SAUCE		
Cream cheese	225g/8oz	1 cup
Single (light) cream	125ml/4floz	½ cup
Salt	1 tsp	1 tsp
Cayenne pepper	¼ tsp	¼ tsp
Seedless raisins	75g/3oz	½ cup

Cut the tops from the peppers and carefully scoop out the pith and seeds, leaving the peppers whole. Set aside. Remove and discard the stems from the tops and chop the flesh into small dice.

Heat the oil in a saucepan. Add the onions, garlic, chillis and diced pepper and fry until they are soft. Add the meat, oregano, salt, bay leaves and Tabasco and fry until the meat loses its pinkness. Stir in the flour, stock, tomato purée (paste) and bring to the boil. Reduce the heat to low, cover the pan and simmer for 30 minutes, stirring occasionally.

Preheat the oven to moderate 180°C (Gas Mark 4, 350°F).

Remove and discard the bay leaves from the beef mixture. Carefully spoon the mixture into the peppers and arrange the peppers in a shallow, well-greased baking dish. Put the dish into the oven and bake for 40 minutes.

Meanwhile, prepare the sauce. Put the cream cheese, cream, salt and cayenne into a small saucepan and simmer gently until the mixture is smooth, stirring constantly. Stir in the seedless raisins and simmer until the sauce is hot but not boiling. Remove from the heat. Pour the sauce over the peppers and cook for a further 15 minutes, or until the sauce is bubbling. Remove from the oven and serve at once.

4 Servings

CHILES EN NOGADA
(Stuffed Peppers with Walnut Cream Sauce)

This exotic dish is traditionally served in Mexico on Independence Day (September 15) because its main ingredients echo the colours of the Mexican flag. In Mexico, California green chillis are used (they can be obtained outside Mexico in cans if they are not available fresh), but green peppers can be substituted, as here, for a more substantial dish.

	Metric/U.K.	U.S.
Large firm green peppers	4	4
Vegetable oil	2 Tbs	2 Tbs
Onion, finely chopped	1	1
Garlic clove, crushed	1	1
Canned peeled tomatoes, drained and chopped	225g/8oz	8oz
Minced (ground) beef	½kg/1lb	1lb
Seedless raisins	3 Tbs	3 Tbs
Ground cinnamon	½ tsp	½ tsp
Ground cloves	½ tsp	½ tsp
Salt and pepper to taste		

Stuffed chillis or green peppers are found in many forms all over Mexico — this particular favourite is from Yucatan where the peppers are stuffed with a spicy minced (ground) beef mixture, then cooked with a sauce of cream cheese and cream.

SAUCE		
Single (light) cream	250ml/8floz	1 cup
Walnuts, shelled and ground	125g/4oz	1 cup
Ground almonds	1 Tbs	1 Tbs
Salt and pepper to taste		
Pomegranate seeds	50g/2oz	⅓ cup

Cut the tops from the peppers and carefully scoop out the pith and seeds, leaving the peppers whole. Cook them in boiling water for 5 minutes, drain and set aside.

Heat the oil in a saucepan. Add the onion and garlic and fry until they are soft. Add the tomatoes and bring to the boil. Stir in the meat until it loses its pinkness. Stir in the raisins, cinnamon, cloves and seasoning and bring to the boil. Reduce the heat to low and simmer the mixture for 10 minutes, or until it is thick and rich.

Preheat the oven to moderate 180°C (Gas Mark 4, 350°F).

Carefully spoon the meat mixture into the green peppers and arrange the peppers in a shallow, well-greased baking dish. Put the dish into the oven and cook for 30 minutes.

Meanwhile, to make the sauce, put the cream, walnuts, almonds and seasoning into a small saucepan. Simmer gently, stirring constantly, until it is hot but not boiling and has thickened.

Remove the dish from the oven and transfer the peppers to a warmed serving dish. Pour over the sauce and scatter over the pomegranate seeds. Serve at once.

4 Servings

HUEVOS A LA FLAMENCA
(Eggs Baked with Sausages, Onions and Pepper)

	Metric/U.K.	U.S.
Olive oil	50ml/2floz	¼ cup
Large onion, chopped	1	1
Garlic clove, crushed	1	1
Red pepper, pith and seeds removed and chopped	1	1
Potatoes, cooked and sliced	2	2
Canned peeled tomatoes	425g/14oz	14oz
Tomato purée (paste)	1 Tbs	1 Tbs
Green peas, weighed after shelling	125g/4oz	⅔ cup
Green beans, chopped	125g/4oz	⅔ cup
Eggs	8	8
Chorizo sausage, cut into 8 slices	125g/4oz	4oz
Serrano ham, cut into strips	125g/4oz	4oz
Canned asparagus tips, drained	225g/8oz	8oz

Heat 3 tablespoons of the oil in a large frying-pan. Add the onion, garlic and pepper and fry until they are soft. Add the potatoes and fry until they are lightly and evenly browned. Stir in the tomatoes and can juice, tomato purée (paste), peas and beans and bring to the boil. Simmer for 5 minutes.

Preheat the oven to moderate 180°C (Gas Mark 4, 350°F).

Spread the tomato mixture over the bottom of a large, shallow baking dish. Make eight hollows in the mixture and carefully break one egg into each one. Garnish around the eggs with the chorizo slices, ham strips and asparagus tips. Pour over the remaining oil. Put the dish into the oven and bake for 20 to 25 minutes, or until the eggs have set and are cooked.

4–8 Servings

Tortilla in Mexico might mean a type of bread made from corn meal but in Spain it describes a thick, flat omelet. This particular basic Tortilla has a filling of potatoes and onion but any vegetables or cooked meat can be used.

TORTILLA
(Basic Omelet)

Tortillas in Mexico are flat breads, usually made from corn meal, but in Spain the same word is used to denote an omelet, somewhat thicker and fuller than the traditional French type. This omelet below has a mixture of potatoes and onions as its filling, a mixture typical of Castile.

	Metric/U.K.	U.S.
Olive oil	2 tsp	2 tsp
Butter	15g/½oz	1 Tbs
Large onion, chopped	1	1
Medium potatoes, cooked and diced	4	4
Chopped parsley	1 Tbs	1 Tbs
Large eggs, lightly beaten	4	4
Salt and pepper to taste		

Heat the oil and butter in a medium omelet or frying-pan. Add the onion and fry until it is golden brown. Add the potatoes and cook for 2 minutes, stirring occasionally. Stir in the parsley. Combine the eggs and seasoning together. Increase the heat to high.

Pour the egg mixture into the pan, tilting it so that the bottom is evenly covered. Reduce the heat to moderate. Using a palette knife or spatula, lift the edges of the omelet and, at the same time, tilt the pan away from you so that the liquid egg escapes from the top and runs on to the pan. Put the pan down flat over the heat and leave until the omelet sets.

Slide the omelet carefully on to a plate, then return to the pan to cook the other side in the same way.

Serve cold.

2–3 Servings

TORTILLA ESPANOLA
(Spanish Omelet)

	Metric/U.K.	U.S.
Olive oil	2 Tbs	2 Tbs
Onion, finely chopped	1	1
Garlic cloves, crushed	3	3
Medium tomatoes, blanched, peeled, seeded and chopped	2	2
Canned pimientos, chopped	6 Tbs	6 Tbs
Eggs	6	6
Salt and pepper to taste		
Milk	1 Tbs	1 Tbs
Frozen green peas, thawed	50g/2oz	⅓ cup

Tortilla Espanola has a classic filling of onion, garlic, tomatoes, pimientos and peas.

Heat the oil in a medium omelet or frying-pan. Add the onion and garlic and fry until they are soft. Stir in the tomatoes and pimientos and fry for a further 3 minutes. Remove the pan from the heat and keep hot. Combine the eggs, seasoning and milk until they are well blended. Stir in the peas.

Preheat the grill (broiler) to high.

Return the pan to the heat and pour the egg mixture into the pan, tilting it so that the bottom is evenly covered. Reduce the heat to low. Using a palette knife or spatula, lift the edges of the omelet and, at the same time, tilt the pan away from you so that the liquid egg escapes from the top and runs on to the pan. Put the pan down flat over the heat until the omelet sets.

Remove the pan from the heat and place it under the grill (broiler). Grill (broil) for 2 minutes, or until the top of the omelet has set. Remove from the heat.

Carefully slide the omelet on to a serving dish and cut into wedges. Serve at once.

3 Servings

Desserts and Cookies

Naranjas al Kirsch is a Spanish dessert of fresh mixed fruit soaked in kirsch.

CALABAZA ENMIELADA
(Sweet Pumpkin)

This is one of the favourite desserts of Mexico. Marrow can be substituted for the pumpkin, if you prefer.

	Metric/U.K.	U.S.
Water	50ml/2floz	4 Tbs
Fresh pumpkin, peeled, and with fibre and seeds removed	1kg/2lb	2lb
Dark brown sugar	275g/10oz	1⅔ cups
Double (heavy) cream, stiffly beaten	250ml/8floz	1 cup

Pour the water into a shallow flameproof casserole, or deep frying-pan. Cut the pumpkin into eight equal pieces and arrange it, in one layer, in the casserole or pan. Sprinkle thickly with the sugar and set the casserole or pan over moderate heat. Bring to the boil. Reduce the heat to low and cover. Simmer for 45 to 50 minutes, basting occasionally or until the pumpkin is tender but still retains its shape.

Remove from the heat and set aside to cool completely. Using a slotted spoon, transfer the pumpkin pieces to a serving dish and spoon over the cooking liquid. Serve at once, garnished with cream.

4 Servings

NARANJAS AL KIRSCH
(Fruit Soaked in Kirsch)

	Metric/U.K.	U.S.
Medium oranges, peeled, pith removed and thinly sliced	6	6
Black cherries, stoned (pitted) and halved	125g/4oz	4oz
Raspberries	225g/8oz	8oz
Castor (superfine) sugar	2 Tbs	2 Tbs
Ground allspice	½ tsp	½ tsp
Flaked almonds	50g/2oz	½ cup
Kirsch	125ml/4floz	½ cup

Put the fruit, in alternating layers, in a medium shallow serving dish, sprinkling a little of the sugar, allspice and flaked almonds over each layer.

Pour over the kirsch. Cover the dish with aluminium foil and place it in the refrigerator. Marinate the fruit for 2 hours, basting occasionally with the kirsch.

Remove the dish from the refrigerator. Remove and discard the foil. Baste once with the kirsch and serve at once.

4 Servings

CAPIROTADA
(Mexican Bread Pudding)

	Metric/U.K.	U.S.
Water	250ml/8floz	1 cup
Dark brown sugar	225g/8oz	1⅓ cups
Ground cinnamon	1½ tsp	1½ tsp
Butter	50g/2oz	4 Tbs
Stale bread, crusts removed and cubed	10 slices	10 slices
Sultanas or seedless raisins	50g/2oz	⅓ cup
Walnuts, chopped	125g/4oz	1 cup
Cottage cheese	175g/6oz	¾ cup
Double (heavy) cream, stiffly beaten	250ml/8floz	1 cup

Put the water, sugar and half the cinnamon into a saucepan and cook over moderate heat, stirring constantly until the sugar has dissolved. Cook the mixture without stirring for 5 minutes.

Meanwhile, melt the butter in a large frying-pan. Add the bread cubes and fry gently until they are evenly browned. Remove from the heat and stir into the syrup mixture. Stir in the raisins, walnuts and cheese and simmer gently until the ingredients are thoroughly blended.

Preheat the oven to fairly hot 190°C (Gas Mark 5, 375°F).

Turn the mixture into a well-greased oven-proof baking dish and sprinkle over the remaining cinnamon. Put the dish into the oven and bake for 15 to 20 minutes, or until the pudding has set and is golden brown. Remove from the heat and serve warm, with the cream.

4 Servings

TORRIJAS
(Bread and Honey Dessert)

	Metric/U.K.	U.S.
White bread, crusts removed and cut into large strips	4 slices	4 slices
Milk	125ml/4floz	½ cup
Egg, lightly beaten	1	1
Butter	25g/1oz	2 Tbs
Clear honey	50ml/2floz	¼ cup
Dry sherry	50ml/2floz	¼ cup

Torrijas is a must for everyone who enjoys heavy, rich puddings — bread and milk soaked with honey and sherry.

Preheat the oven to warm 170°C (Gas Mark 3, 325°F).

Arrange the bread in a shallow dish and

Quesadillas can be a multitude of things in Mexican cooking — there is a dish of deep-fried stuffed tortillas which can be so called but it also refers to this delightful snack cake made from crisp pastry with a cheese and raisin filling.

	Metric/U.K.	U.S.
beaten	2	2
Iced water	3–4 Tbs	3–4 Tbs
Milk	2 Tbs	2 Tbs
Sugar	2 Tbs	2 Tbs
FILLING		
Cottage cheese, strained	225g/8oz	1 cup
Egg, beaten with 2 egg yolks	1	1
Castor (superfine) sugar	125g/4oz	½ cup
Mixed spice or ground allspice	⅛ tsp	⅛ tsp
Currants	75g/3oz	½ cup
Lemon juice	1 tsp	1 tsp .
Vanilla essence (extract)	¼ tsp	¼ tsp

pour over the milk. Set aside to soak for 4 minutes. Using a slotted spoon, transfer the bread to kitchen towels to drain. Dip the bread into the beaten egg, then set aside on a plate.

Melt the butter in a flameproof casserole. Add the bread and cook until it is lightly and evenly browned. Meanwhile, combine the honey and sherry. Pour into the casserole.

Put the casserole into the oven and bake for 20 to 25 minutes, or until the bread is golden brown. Remove from the oven and serve at once, or set aside to cool completely before serving.

2–3 Servings

QUESADILLAS
(Mexican Cheese Squares)

	Metric/U.K.	U.S.
PASTRY		
Flour	350g/12oz	3 cups
Salt	¼ tsp	¼ tsp
Butter, chilled	175g/6oz	12 Tbs
Small eggs, lightly		

Sift the flour and salt into a bowl. Add the butter and cut it into small pieces with a knife. With your fingertips, rub the butter into the flour until the mixture resembles fine breadcrumbs. Add the beaten eggs with 2 tablespoons of the iced water and mix into the flour mixture with the knife. Add more water if the dough is too dry. Knead the dough gently and form into a ball. Wrap in foil and chill in the refrigerator for 30 minutes.

Preheat the oven to fairly hot 200°C (Gas Mark 6, 400°F).

To make the filling, beat the ingredients together until they are well blended.

Remove the dough from the refrigerator and divide it in half. Roll out one-half of the dough on a lightly floured surface, to a rectangle large enough to line a 18cm/7in by 28cm/11in baking sheet. Lift the dough on a rolling pin and place over the sheet. Spoon over the filling, spreading it to within about ½cm/¼in of the edges. Using a pastry brush, moisten the edges of the dough with a little water.

Roll the remaining dough out to a rectangle large enough to cover the filling. Lift the dough on to the filling, pressing the edges together to seal. Cut a slit in the centre of the dough and trim the edges. Discard the trimmings. Using a pastry brush, brush the top of the dough with the milk and sprinkle over the sugar.

Put the baking sheet into the oven and bake the dough for 20 to 25 minutes, or until it is golden brown. Remove from the oven and set aside to cool completely. Using a sharp knife, cut the pastry into eight squares and serve.

8 Pastries

TORTAS DE ACEITE
(Sesame Seed and Aniseed Biscuits [Cookies])

	Metric/U.K.	U.S.
Vegetable oil	350ml/12floz	1½ cups
Thinly pared rind of ½ lemon		
Sesame seeds	1 Tbs	1 Tbs
Aniseed	1 Tbs	1 Tbs
Dry white wine	125ml/4floz	½ cup
Finely grated lemon rind	2 tsp	2 tsp
Finely grated orange rind	2 tsp	2 tsp
Sugar	125g/4oz	½ cup
Flour	575g/1¼lb	5 cups
Ground cinnamon	1 tsp	1 tsp
Ground cloves	1 tsp	1 tsp
Ground ginger	1 tsp	1 tsp
Flaked almonds	25g/1oz	¼ cup

Heat the oil in a saucepan. When it is hot, add the pared lemon rind, sesame seeds and ani-seed and remove the pan from the heat. Set aside and leave to cool. Using a slotted spoon, remove the lemon rind. Pour the oil mixture into a large bowl and add the wine, lemon and orange rind and sugar, beating until all the ingredients are well blended.

Sift the flour and spices into a bowl. Gradually add the mixture to the oil mixture, beating with a wooden spoon until they form a stiff dough. Using your hands, lightly knead the dough until it is smooth. Form into a ball and wrap in greaseproof or waxed paper. Set aside at room temperature for 30 minutes.

Preheat the oven to fairly hot 200°C (Gas Mark 6, 400°F). Line two large baking sheets with non-stick silicone paper.

Remove the paper from the dough and divide the dough into 24 equal pieces. Roll the pieces into small balls and, using the palm of your hand, flatten them into flat round biscuits (cookies), about 1cm/½in thick. Arrange the biscuits (cookies) on the prepared sheets and press a few flaked almonds into the top of each one.

Put the sheets into the oven and bake for 15 to 20 minutes, or until the biscuits (cookies) are firm to the touch and golden brown around the edges. Remove the sheets from the oven

Spicy flavourful biscuits (cookies) filled with sesame seeds and aniseed — Tortas de Aceite.

and transfer the biscuits (cookies) to a wire rack to cool. Allow to cool completely before serving.

24 biscuits (cookies)

TURRON
(Almond Sweets [Candies])

	Metric/U.K.	U.S.
Blanched almonds, toasted	450g/1lb	4 cups
Sugar	225g/8oz	1 cup
Clear honey	125ml/4floz	½ cup
MARZIPAN		
Ground almonds	50g/2oz	½ cup
Icing (confectioners') sugar	40g/1½oz	⅓ cup
Sugar	15g/½oz	1½ Tbs
Egg yolk	½	½
Dash of almond essence (extract)		

To make the marzipan, sift the almonds, icing (confectioners') sugar and sugar into a bowl. Mix lightly together. Gradually beat in the egg yolk and almond essence (extract), using a knife or a spatula to stir them in. Lightly dust a working surface with icing (confectioners') sugar. Turn the marzipan mixture out on to the working surface and knead it, pressing down and away from you with the heel of your hand, for 5 minutes or until the mixture is very smooth. Set the marzipan aside.

Combine the almonds, sugar and honey in a large saucepan and set the pan over very low heat. Cook the mixture until the sugar has dissolved, stirring constantly. Increase the heat to moderate and bring to the boil. Cook for 3 minutes, stirring constantly. Remove the pan from the heat and stir in the marzipan. Beat the mixture until the ingredients are thoroughly combined.

Spoon the mixture into a well-greased 15cm/6in by 23cm/9in baking pan, and set aside to cool slightly. Mark the mixture into 4cm/1½in squares and leave aside to cool completely.

Remove the sweets (candies) from the pan and break them into squares. Either place the sweets (candies) on a serving plate, or wrap them in greaseproof or waxed paper and store until required.

About 24 sweets (candies)

CHURROS
(Fried Choux Pastries)

	Metric/U.K.	U.S.
Sufficient vegetable oil for deep-frying		
Icing (confectioners') sugar, sifted		
CHOUX PASTRY		
Water	150ml/5floz	⅝ cup
Butter, cut into small pieces	40g/1½oz	3 Tbs
Salt	½ tsp	½ tsp
Pinch of grated nutmeg		
Flour	150g/5oz	1¼ cups
Medium eggs	3	3

First make the pastry. Bring the water to the boil over moderate heat. Add the butter, salt and nutmeg. When the butter has melted,

remove the pan from the heat and beat in the flour. Continue beating until the mixture pulls away from the sides of the pan.

One by one, beat the eggs into the mixture, beating each one into the dough until it is well blended before adding the next. When the eggs have all been completely absorbed, the mixture should be thick and somewhat glossy. Set aside to cool. Spoon the dough into a piping bag with a 1cm/½in plain nozzle.

Fill a large saucepan one-third full with oil and heat until it reaches 180°C (350°F) on a deep-fat thermometer, or until a small cube of stale bread dropped into the oil turns golden in 55 seconds.

Holding the piping bag in your left hand, squeeze out 20cm/8in lengths of the dough into the hot oil, cutting the lengths with scissors. Do not cook more than two or three lengths at a time. Deep-fry the pastries for about 8 minutes, or until they are crisp and golden brown. Using a slotted spoon, carefully remove the churros from the oil and drain on kitchen towels.

Sprinkle with icing (confectioners') sugar and serve hot. Or set aside to cool, sprinkle with icing (confectioners') sugar and serve cold.

4 Servings

FIGOS RELLENOS
(Stuffed Figs)

These delicious little sweetmeats are eloquent testimony to the North African influence on Spanish cuisine. They are usually eaten after the meal, perhaps with coffee or tea.

	Metric/U.K.	U.S.
Dried figs, stalks removed	24	24
Ground almonds	125g/4oz	⅔ cup
Sultanas or seedless raisins	50g/2oz	⅓ cup
Dark cooking (semi-sweet) chocolate, grated	25g/1oz	1 square
Orange-flavoured liqueur	3 Tbs	3 Tbs
Whole blanched almonds, toasted	24	24

Preheat the oven to moderate 180°C (Gas Mark 4, 350°F).

Holding a fig in one hand, push your thumb into the hole at the top and rotate the fig so that the centre becomes hollowed out. Combine the ground almonds, sultanas or raisins, chocolate and liqueur.

Using one teaspoonful at a time, fill the hollowed figs with the almond mixture. When the figs are full, gently press the tops together with your fingertips.

Arrange the figs, open end up, in a 23cm/9in round baking pan or shallow casserole. Put the pan or casserole into the oven and bake for 10 minutes, or until the tops of the figs open a little. Remove the figs from the oven. Insert a whole almond halfway into the hole in each fig.

Set the stuffed figs aside to cool completely before serving.

24 Sweetmeats

Glossary

Chilli peppers: There are literally scores of different varieties of chilli pepper regularly used in Mexican cooking, from the reasonably mild to the suicidally hot. Many are interchangeable with one another, and in this book, the types recommended in specific recipes have been limited to those available outside Mexico. In general, when seeding or chopping chillis, care should be taken to wear gloves and to rinse the chillis in cold, running water—they can be very hot, and if the seeds particularly come into contact with skin, they can cause an unpleasant, burning sensation. The major types of chillis are:
Ancho, a mild, dark capsicum, usually obtained dried from Mexican food stores. They are much less hot than most of the others on the market and if they are to be substituted for any other type, the quantity should be doubled to obtain the equivalent hotness of taste.
California, usually sold in cans from Mexican or Spanish food stores. They are fairly mild, smooth skinned and green and are often sold merely as 'green chillis'. They are the peppers used traditionally in Chiles Relleños. They can be stored, in their can liquid, in a screw-top container in the refrigerator for up to one month.
Jalapeño, usually sold in cans from Mexican or Spanish food stores. They are smooth skinned, green and very hot indeed. Care should be taken when chopping or otherwise handling them. They can be stored, in their can liquid, in a screw-top container in the refrigerator for up to one month.
Small dried red, usually known in Mexico as the *hontaka* chilli. They are native to Japan but widely used in cooking all over Latin America. They are very hot. Usually bought in bags or small portions and can be stored dry indefinitely.
Péquin, as above, small dried red chillis somewhat similar in appearance to the *hontaka*. They are very hot indeed. Can sometimes be obtained from Mexican food stores but can be difficult to obtain outside Mexico. When unobtainable, substitute other small dried hot red chillis, such as *hontaka*.

Chorizo sausage: a coarse red sausage, obtainable from Spanish food stores or good quality delicatessens. There are several varieties, but usually one type can be substituted for another. If chorizo is unobtainable, Italian *pepperoni* sausage, which is somewhat similar in texture, can be substituted, or any type of garlic sausage.

Coriander leaves: used as a condiment in Mexican cooking. Available fresh from Mexican, Greek or Indian food stores, or parsley can be used as a substitute. Coriander leaves can also be grown from coriander seeds. Plant in pots, keep indoors in a warm place and water frequently until it flowers.

Morcilla sausage: a smoked blood sausage, very popular in Spain, especially as a soup ingredient. Obtainable from Spanish food stores. Any type of blood sausage can be substituted if morcilla is unobtainable.

Pine nuts: a popular ingredient in Spanish cooking, especially dishes with a Catalan origin. Available from health food stores or delicatessens. If unavailable, hazelnuts or even finely chopped walnuts or pecans may be substituted.

Pomegranate seeds: the bright red dried seeds of the pomegranate fruit, sometimes used as a garnish in Mexican cooking. Available from Mexican or Indian food stores.

Salt cod: a specially cured form of cod fillet vastly popular in Spain and all other parts of the Mediterranean. Usually obtainable from Spanish and some French food stores, or some speciality fish merchants. If unavailable, cod or any white fish fillets can be substituted—although in this case the initial soaking stage should be omitted.

Serrano ham: a specially smoked ham, eaten uncooked, popular all over Spain. Available from Spanish food stores, but difficult and expensive to obtain outside Spain. If unavailable, *prosciutto*, or any other type of smoked ham may be substituted.

Tomatillo verde: small green, rather piquant tomatoes, usually sold canned, and a very popular ingredient in Mexican cooking. There is really no substitute, but if unavailable the texture may be duplicated by using canned peeled Italian plum tomatoes. The taste, however, is not the same.